LAO TZU'S
TAO TE CHING

Psychotherapeutic
Commentaries

LAO TZU'S
TAO TE CHING
Psychotherapeutic Commentaries

A WAYFARING COUNSELOR'S RENDERING

OF

THE TAO VIRTUOSITY EXPERIENCE

Raymond Bart Vespe

REGENT PRESS
Berkeley, California

Paperback
ISBN 13: 978-1-58790-367-0
ISBN 10: 1-58790-367-7

E-book:
ISBN 13: 978-1-58790-368-7
ISBN 10: 1-58790-368-7

Library of Congress Control Number: 2016949806

SECOND CORRECTED PRINTING 2017

Manufactured in the United States of America

REGENT PRESS
www.regentpress.net
regentpress@mindspring.com

CONTENTS

DEDICATION

For my parents, Benjamin Richard and Anne Agnes Vespe; my brother, Benjamin Richard Vespe Jr.; my daughters, Laura Anne Wilson, Cheryl Jean Tassa and Arianna Selene Lewin; and my grandchildren, Grant Walter and Shannon Casey Wilson; Ilanit Allison, Liana Carmel and Oren Ethan Tassa and Avery Anthony Lewin; with deep gratitude and respect for who you are and for the precious opportunity to experience what it is and what it means to be a son, brother, father and grandfather; for compassionately and tolerantly bearing the transient sorrows of conditioned love and for wholeheartedly and intimately sharing the lasting joys of unconditioned love.

ACKNOWLEDGEMENTS

Of my students, trainees and supervisees; patients, counselees and clients and teachers, therapists and colleagues for the precious opportunity and the shared experiences of Soulfully contributing to each others' personal growth, professional development and Spiritual evolution. When committed to learning, healing and awakening; everyone and everything educates, transforms and enlightens.

Of my son-in-law, Ashley Evan Lewin and youngest daughter, Arianna Selene Lewin, for helping me to overcome a technophobic relationship with a laptop computer and to learn how to use it for word processing this rendition.

Of Ralph Metzner, Ph.D. for a long-standing collegial association and friendship and for directing me to his publisher, Mark Weiman of Regent Press, without whose creative genius and skillful midwifing during the last trimester of the pregnancy, a Petocin-free labor and epidural-free delivery would not have happened and the present work would not have been birthed into being naturally.

LAO	TZU
老	子
OLD	BOY
AGED	CHILD
EXPERIENCED	SON
ESTABLISHED	GENTLEMAN
WELL-COOKED	PHILOSOPHER
VENERABLE	MASTER

THE OLD BOY/PHILOSOPHER/MASTER.
TERMS OF GREAT HONOR/DEEP RESPECT/HIGH REGARD
FOR LAO TZU, THE PURPORTED AUTHOR OF THE
TAO TE CHING TEXT.[1]

PROLOGUE

In China sometime during the 6th-5th Century BCE, an elderly human being riding an ox is approaching one of the frontier passes opening westward toward India, Tibet, the Gobi Desert and the K'un Lun mountain range. The keeper of the pass, Yin Hsi, recognizing that this individual is an old sage/philosopher (Lao Tzu) and may have some wisdom to share, asks several questions before allowing passage.

YH 'What is Tao?'

LT (Waves his hands in a sweeping circle all around him).

YH 'What is Te?'

LT (Points the index fingers of both hands toward his chest and gently taps his heart area).

YH 'What is Ch'i?'

LT (With palms up, raises his arms toward the sky; with palms down lowers his arms toward the earth and back and forth between them).

YH 'What is Yin/Yang?'

LT (Opens and closes both hands and clasps and releases them).

YH 'What is Wu Wei?'

LT (Extends both arms outward and swings them from left to right and right to left in a figure eight motion).

YH 'What is Tzu Jan?'

LT (Jumps up and down and dances all around).

YH 'What is Wan Wu?'

LT (Reaches down, picks up several stones, twigs and leaves and tosses them all around).

YH 'Who are Sheng Jen?'

LT (Points the index finger of his right hand toward Yin Hsi, nods his head up and down and bows slowly).

YH (Bowing) 'Thank you. You have answered all of my questions without speaking a word just like a wise sage would do. Where, may I ask, are you heading?'

LT (Smiling) 'To the K'un Lun mountains of immortality.'

YH 'Why is it that you are leaving our splendid country, the Celestial Empire, the Middle Kingdom, the center of the entire world?'

LT 'I am heartbroken over its political intrigues, power hungry leaders and social upheaval. Soon there will be bloody warfare between states. It is my time to leave. A wandering individual named Chuang Chou will be coming along and telling stories about how true human beings can find freedom and happiness living amidst such carnage.'

Lao Tzu's silent answers to Yin Hsi's questions confirm his intuitive sense that Lao Tzu is in fact a Sacred and wise human being and prompts him to ask Lao Tzu:

YH (Bowing) 'Before passing through, I am beseeching you to impart some of your wisdom which I will respectfully, dutifully and accurately record for the benefit of all human beings who are here now and who will follow.'

LT 'Your humility and sincerity are to be honored and your request is to be complied with. Yes, most certainly!'

And so Lao Tzu speaks and Yin Hsi inks the wise sayings on bamboo slips which he later bundles together after Lao Tzu's passage. This wisdom, written in approximately 5,000 Chinese characters, has since come down to us for over 2,000 years as the *Tao Te Ching* text.

INTRODUCTION

Authorship

It is unclear whether the *Tao Te Ching* text is authored by a single individual named Lao Tzu or is a compilation of orally transmitted wisdom sayings made over time. The former position is associated with the following legendary biography of Lao Tzu.

Lao Tzu is born sometime during the 6th Century BCE. He is variously named Li Erh, Lao Tan and Lao Tzu/old boy/philosopher/Master. Lao Tzu is an archivist in the royal court of the Later/Eastern Chou dynasty (c. 770-221 BCE) located in the feudal State of Ch'u (c. 740-330 BCE) in Southern China. This is a time, the Spring/Ch'un and Autumn/Ch'iu period (c. 770-475 BCE), of socio-political upheaval, division and disintegration prior to the Warring States/Chan Kuo period (c. 475-221 BCE), a time of eventual bloody internecine warfare being waged by feudal rulers vying for hegemony.

Disheartened, Lao Tzu mounts an ox and commences to leave China, heading westward toward India, Tibet and the Gobi Desert. At Han Ku Kuan/Gobi desert valley frontier pass, he meets Kuan Yin Hsi, guardian of the frontier pass, who, recognizing Lao Tzu's sageliness, asks him to share his wisdom before passing on through. Lao Tzu complies and his sayings are recorded on bamboo slips in approximately five-thousand Chinese characters. Following this, Lao Tzu continues on heading westward to the K'un Lun mountain range, the axis of the world and abode of immortal beings.

The legend of Lao Tzu is a beautiful metaphor for the human experience of developing wisdom; disengaging from socio-cultural, interpersonal and/or intrapsychic conflicts; transmitting this wisdom for the benefit of human beings and ultimately transitioning through elevated frontier passageways to timeless realms.

Text

The *Tao Te Ching* is the principal text of the ancient Chinese philosophical/Spiritual tradition of Taoism and is the most widely translated book in world literature next to the Holy Bible. Regardless of the veracity of the intriguing mythology and/or historical biography surrounding Lao Tzu, we have inherited an actual document containing quintessential wisdom which is, and has been, a perennial classic, adaptable to, and relevant for, each new age in a wide variety of differing cultures.

The precise dating of the *Tao Te Ching* text is not determined. Over time, the text, originally titled *The Book of Lao Tzu*, becomes titled the *Tao Te Ching* and its passages are divided into eighty-one in two sections, the Tao Ching (passages 1-37) and the Te Ching (passages 38-81).

Relatively recent archaeological excavations have unearthed two silk manuscripts of the *Te Tao Ching* (the order being reversed) dating from c. 168-206 BCE at Mawangdui in 1973 and unbundled bamboo slips dating from c. 300 BCE at Guodian in 1993. Both of these materials are predating the standard received text commentaried upon by Wang Pi (c. 226-249 CE) and used for most translations.

Language

Chinese language characters in their ancient origins, shamanic roots and seal writing; visually represent objects with graphic symbols that look like what they depict. Over time, the original characters change due to the developments of written language; transcription errors, phonetic variations, commentator interpolations and differences in writing mediums and instruments, e.g., carving in wood, stone and jade; etching on oracle bones, tortoise shells and bronze; lacquering on bamboo slips and inking on silk and paper. A sharp metal stylus on a solid clay tablet is producing a very different shaped character than a soft bristle brush on absorbant rice paper.

Chinese characters are etymologically composed of radicals and phonetics which are enabling their use in spoken and written language as well as giving them deeper, associated and more extended meaning. The Chinese characters do not distinguish nouns and verbs; past, present and future tense; active and passive voice and feminine and masculine gender. This presents translators with difficulties in achieving literal accuracy as well as opportunities for creative interpretations.

In this rendition; in the interests of facilitating a sense of universality, gender equality, immediacy and ongoingness; the following grammatical forms are being used:

1) plural personal pronouns: we/us/our/they/them/their.

2) present tense/active voice: is/am/are.

3) gerunds/verbs used as nouns: by adding -ing.

4) the verb 'being' preceding/modifying some nouns/verbs. e.g.,

'The teacher instructs the student' is changed to 'Teachers are instructing students.'

'Philosophy benefits people' is changed to 'Philosophizing is benefiting human beings.'

'Freedom is limited by conventionality' is changed to 'Being free is being limited by being conventional.'

'The sage is wise. He lets things be' is changed to 'Sages are being wise. They are letting beings be.'

Terms

In this rendition, some of the designations typically found in *Tao Te Ching* translations are being combined and named as follows:

❖ *'people'* for the general public and lesser developed human beings.

❖ *'human beings'* for greater developed human beings who are conscious of Tao.

❖ *'most developed'* for human beings, states or qualities regarded as greatest, highest, deepest, fullest and most evolved or complete.

❖ *'rulers'/'leaders'* for kings, princes, dukes, lords, barons, etc..

❖ *'wise human beings'* for Sacred/wise human beings who are embodying, personifying and identifying *as* the characteristics, qualities and activities of Tao.

❖ *'embodying', 'internalizing', 'assimilating', 'personifying' or 'enacting' Tao* for embracing, grasping, according with, clinging to, attaining and/or realizing Tao.

❖ *'identifying as Tao'* for returning to and uniting with Tao, being Tao-like and *being*-Tao; the nondual/integral state of unity and identity with the totality of everyone/everything.

Concepts

There are numerous philosophical concepts of ancient Chinese Taoism found throughout the *Tao Te Ching* text. The following eight are principal ones used in this rendition and its synopses, commentaries and applications. The Chinese characters and further descriptions of these experiential concepts are interspersed throughout the rendition.

Tao	Ultimate Reality; Absolute, Infinite and Eternal Constant; Nondual, Essential and Transcendent Unity; All That Is As It Is.[2]
Ch'i	The primordial and acquired life-giving and sustaining vital energy and life force and the cosmic Spirit of Tao in/as everything everywhere in the universe.[3]

Te	The inner Tao-nature, unique individu-alizing, efficacious potency and Virtuosity of everything.[4]
Yin/Yang Ch'i	Shady/sunny; the dynamic bipolar energies of Tao continually alternating, counterbal-ancing and reversing to their complement.[5/7]
Wu Wei Ch'i	No 'thing'-doing / Nothing 'doing'; the kinetic flowing energies of Tao continuously circulat-ing, cycling and returning to their origin.[6/7]
Tzu Jan	Self so-ness; the natural, spontaneous and free presencing of everything just as it is.[8]
Wan Wu	All beings; the myriad, diverse and objectified totality of everything *as* immanent Tao.[8]
Sheng Jen	Sacred/wise human beings who are embody-ing, personifying and identifying *as* Tao/Ch'i, being Tao/Ch'i-like and *being* Tao/Ch'i.[9]

To succinctly sum up these eight principal experiential concepts:

A constant *Ultimate Reality* (*Tao*) *as* its consistent *vital energy* (Ch'i) is continually dynamically *polarizing/reversing* (*Yin/Yang Ch'i*), continuously kinetically *flowing/returning* (*Wu Wei Ch'i*), coherently uniquely *individualizing* (*Te*) and creatively spontaneously *presencing* (*Tzu Jan*) as the complete phenomenal *actuality/totality* (*Wan Wu*) of experience in the awakened heart-minds and conscious awareness of *Sacred/wise human beings* (*Sheng Jen*) who are *embodying/personifying /identifying as Tao/Ch'i* and its characteristics, qualities and activities.[10/11]

States

The *Tao Te Ching* text includes the following four principal Wu/Nonbeing and Yu/Being States, their characteristics, associated concepts and end states:

WU STATE
Wu Chih
Non-knowing
No-'thing' knowing
Knowing no-'things'
No-thing/Tao 'knowing'
Not mental object-contents
Not construing/interpreting
Not abstracting/analyzing
Not defining/naming
Not classifying/categorizing

YU STATE
Letting-Be
Conceptless/clearness
Recognizing/receiving
Not rejecting/revising
Acknowledging/accepting
Comprehending

CONCEPT
Te
Individualized/unique
Inner truth/enlightened
Empowerment/efficacy
Virtuosity

END STATE
Sanity/sagacity
Not ignorance
Truth/trueness
Integrity/wisdom

WU STATE
Wu Yu
Non-having
No-'thing' having
Having no-'things'
No-thing/Tao 'having'
Not emotional object-goods
Not investing/evaluating
Not attaching/acquiring
Not claiming/owning
Not storing/displaying

YU STATE
Letting-Go
Desireless/emptiness
Reflecting/releasing
Not refracting/retaining
Attuning/according
Counterbalancing

CONCEPT
Yin/Yang Ch'i
Bipolar/complementary
Alternating/balancing
Centering/voiding
Reversing

END STATE
Simplicity/sufficiency
Not attachment
Good/goodness
Beauty/harmony

WU STATE
Wu Wei
Non-doing
No-'thing' doing
Doing no-'things'
No-thing/Tao 'doing'
Not volitional object-deeds
Not planning/strategizing
Not asserting/administrating
Not implementing/executing
Not controlling/forcing

YU STATE
Going-With
Purposeless/stillness
Responding/replying
Not resisting/reacting
Allowing/accompanying
Cooperating

CONCEPT
Wu Wei Ch'i
Yielding/flowing
Complying/following
Circulating/cycling
Returning

END STATE
Support/synergy
Not error
Right/rightness
Grace/peace

WU STATE
Wu Yu
Non-being
No-'thing' being
Being no-'things'
No-thing/Tao 'being'
Not relational object-others
Not separating/dividing
Not alienating/abandoning
Not distancing/isolating
Not stereotyping/excluding

YU STATE
Being-With
Relationless/oneness
Rejoining/reuniting
Not reducing/removing
Affiliating/allying
Communing

CONCEPT
Tao
Joining/participating
Sharing/community
Unity/identity
Residing

END STATE
Sacredness/splendor
Not separation
Reality/realness
Completion/freedom

Concepts and States

The following further identifies and correlates the four principal experiential concepts of Te, Yin/Yang Ch'i, Wu Wei Ch'i and Tao and their respective Wu/Nonbeing and Yu/Being States:

TE

❖ not only analyzing/categorizing/defining/labeling.

❖ not externalizing/abstracting/construing awarenesses into mental 'thing-contents' in order to conceive/identify/comprehend/understand/'know' some 'thing'.

❖ letting-be/mental clearness/truth/wisdom/uniqueness.

❖ noticing/witnessing/beholding.

❖ attending/accepting/acknowledging/appreciating/not avoiding/altering.

❖ regarding/respecting/receiving/realizing/not rejecting/revising.

❖ comprehending/concentrating/contemplating/not conjuring/concluding.

❖ sanity/sagacity/singularity/not scrutinizing/surmising/stipulating.

❖ individuality/integrity/authenticity/Virtuosity/potency/efficacy.

❖ uniqueness/wiseness/kindness.

YIN/YANG CH'I

❖ not only evaluating/preferring/judging/investing.

❖ not wanting/desiring/coveting experiences into emotional 'thing-goods' in order to pursue/acquire/claim/possess/'have' some 'thing'.

❖ letting-go/emotional emptiness/good/beauty/harmony.

❖ balancing/centralizing/voiding.

❖ attuning/adjusting/according/alternating/not assessing/attaching.

❖ relinquishing/reflecting/reciprocating/reversing/not refracting/retaining.

❖ corresponding/complementing/compensating/not counteracting/conflicting.

❖ suitability/simplicity/sufficiency/not seeking/selecting/storing.

❖ bipolarity/complementarity/mutuality/equality/reciprocity/impartiality.

❖ equalness/fairness/goodness.

Wu Wei Ch'i

❖ not only planning/goal-setting/strategizing/directing.

❖ not contriving/devising/interfering/forcing activities into volitional 'thing-deeds' in order to fabricate/engineer/implement/execute/'do' some 'thing'.

❖ going-with/volitional stillness/right/grace/peace.

❖ yielding/following/flowing.

❖ allowing/acceding/affirming/accompanying/not asserting/aggressing.

❖ resonating/responding/replying/reinforcing/not resisting/reacting.

❖ conforming/complying/cooperating/not controlling/contending.

❖ sourcing/supporting/synergy/not striving/stressing/struggling.

❖ activity/originality/flexibility/fluidity/facility/agency/efficiency.

❖ softness/gentleness/rightness.

TAO

- ❖ not only self-containing/independence/autonomy/ freedom.

- ❖ not separating/dividing/fragmenting interconnections into relational 'thing-others' in order to exist/become/ live/'be' some 'one'.

- ❖ being-with/relational oneness/reality/unity/identity.

- ❖ joining/participating/uniting.

- ❖ associating/affiliating/allying/abiding/not alienating/ abandoning.

- ❖ rotating/revolving/returning/residing/not restricting/ restraining.

- ❖ connecting/committing/communing/not constricting/constraining.

- ❖ sociability/Sacredness/splendor/not severing/stereotyping/suppressing.

- ❖ amiability/multiplicity/unity/community/identity/ intimacy/ultimacy.

- ❖ oneness/wholeness/allness.

Metaphors

While not explicitly focused on in this rendition, the various terms and concepts in the *Tao Te Ching* can be understood metaphorically and inwardly, as well as literally and outwardly, and can be 'translated' and applied to your own experience as you read through the passages, e.g.,

The 'kingdom' — our personal world of human being, existing and experiencing; our life as a whole.

The 'people' — all of our various subordinate ego-identities, self-images and concepts, subpersonalities and 'me's'.

The socially conditioned, conventionally accepted, ego-identified and least developed 'self' of consensus reality and ordinary experience.

The '10,000 things' — all of the myriad object-contents focused on in our conscious awareness, field of ordinary experience and phenomenal world.

The 'ruler' — our principal ego-identity, executive and observing ego, the 'I' who thinks that it creates, generates, organizes, regulates, maintains and enacts oneself.

The 'wise human being' — our truest, deepest, highest, fullest and most completely awakened, developed and actualized Self. The transpersonal, archetypal, integral and Tao-identified Self.

The 'State' — Pure, Cosmic and Supramental Consciousness. Nondual Reality, Integral Being and Tao-Being.

'Tao' — the above State that is Ultimate Reality, All That Is / As It Is absolutely and essentially independent of any and all conditions, limitations and influences of people, rulers and wise human beings.

'Earth' — our terrestrial and embodied Tao-nature. The elemental, physical, instinctual, animal and natural dimensions of human being, existence, consciousness and experience.

'Heaven' — our celestial and inSpirited Tao-nature. The supramental, Spiritual, rational, divine and cultural dimensions of human being, existence, consciousness and experience.

'Warring States' — any and all dualistic intrapsychic conflicts between various subordinate egos and any and all interpersonal conflicts between ourselves and others. Discrete egos vying for dominant authority and control in our personality.

'Middle Kingdom' — Human Being as the center of Heaven-Earth. Heart as the center of belly-head. The balancing, centering and integrating of bipolarities within being, existence, consciousness and experience. The Axis, Pivot and Heart of Tao, the vital core of human being/living in the middle energy center of the human body.

Experiences

The cast of characters in the literal, outer and exoteric experiential theater of the *Tao Te Ching* is composed of unnamed rulers and leaders, wise and fully developed human beings and masses of typically least developed and least wise people. The wise human beings are advising the rulers and leaders on ways of being and ways of ordering their kingdoms and governing the people.

And the cast of characters in the metaphorical, inner and esoteric experiential theater of the *Tao Te Ching* is comprised of principal executive ego-selves, wise and fully developed Tao-Selves and numerous typically least wise and least developed egos. The Tao-Selves are advising the primary executive egos on ways of being and ways of harmonizing their worlds and regulating their subordinate egos.

Understood metaphorically, the *Tao Te Ching* is a guiding instructional and operational manual for Self-awakening, self-transformative experiencing and returning to our original, most essential, innermost, deepest, centermost, truest, utmost and wisest nature *as* Tao. These transformative experiences can be seen in the following transitions:

❖ From least wise and least developed people to most wise and most developed human beings.

❖ From identifying with egos to identifying *as* Tao-Selves.

❖ From ego-images and self-concepts to Tao-States of Being.

❖ From unreal/false/counterfeit/inauthentic ego-selves to real/true/genuine/authentic Tao-Selves.

❖ From mundane existences, lives, relationships and

experiences to their Mysterious origination, Miraculous formations, Marvelous manifestations and Magnificent completions.

❖ From being asleep, alienated and lost as a conditioned and bound ego-object in a collective world of 'things' and 'others' to being awake, interrelated and at home as an unconditioned and free Tao-Self in a universal community of Beings and Human Beings.

Commentaries

There are hundreds of commentaries on the *Tao Te Ching* made during a period of over one-thousand five hundred years. Typically, they are made from some particular perspective, e.g., political, martial, philosophical, mystical, religious, alchemical, medical, yogic, etc.. The present commentaries are psychotherapeutically-oriented and demonstrate how some Chinese Taoist ways of being can be applied in the practice of psychotherapy/ counseling in ways that are relevant, meaningful, useful and beneficial to the human beings engaged in it.

The commentaries are not only intended for professional psychotherapists/counselors but also for anyone who is interested in integrating the wisdom of the *Tao Te Ching* and their experiences of human being, living and relating.

On Attending

In the commentaries of this rendition, instead of being named psychotherapists/counselors, the human beings conducting the practice of psychotherapy/counseling are designated as 'wise attenders' and psychotherapy/counseling is designated as the 'attending relationship/process'. This is consistent with the etymological meaning of psychotherapy as 'Soul' (Greek

– psyche) 'attending' (Greek - therapeuein) and also is identical with Sheng Jen/wise human beings nourishing, cultivating and sustaining Tao as our innermost, deepest, centermost, truest and utmost nature, i.e., Te/Virtuosity.

Attending is a fundamental quality and essential factor in the psychotherapy/counseling relationship/process.[12] Also, various forms and meanings of 'attending' denote states and activities of being and consciousness that apply to four principal experiential concepts identified in this rendition, integrating them and psychotherapy/counseling practice in the following ways:

TE

❖ in the letting-be/'knowing' mode of no-'thing' knowing *about*, or the construing *of*, mental object-contents.

❖ paying attention to/mindfully, availably and receptively observing/giving focused heed to the phenomena of/in conscious awareness.

YIN/YANG CH'I

❖ in the letting-go/'having' mode of no-'thing' having *of*, or the attaching *to*, emotional object-'goods'.

❖ being attentive to/thoughtfully, sympathetically and kindly considering/caring about/empathizing with the needs/comfort of others.

WU WEI CH'I

❖ in the going-with/'doing' mode of no-'thing' doing *of*, or the performing *of*, volitional object-'deeds'.

❖ attending to/responsively, cooperatively and appropriately taking care of necessities requiring completing.

TAO

❖ the being-with/'being' mode of no-'thing' being *of*, or the separating *of*, relational object-'others'.

❖ being an attender or an attendant present at/collectively joining/participating in a given place/occasion/event or looking after/staying with another as a companion/ friend/professional or being concomitant to/associated with/resultant of circumstances.

Also, the various meanings of 'tending' have to do with awaiting, standing by, listening, watching over, caring for, serving, cultivating and fostering.

Wise psychotherapists/counselors are human beings who are paying attention, being attentive and attending *to* as an attender present *at*, ready to serve and participating *in* the attending relationship/process and the attendant phenomena concomitantly associated with and accompanying it.

Ideally, these ways of wise attending in psychotherapy/ counseling involve the mental clearness, emotional emptiness, volitional stillness and relational oneness of psychotherapists/ counselors and the human beings with whom they are working. These ways of attending can open the Way to co-creating and co-experiencing the unique individuality, equal reciprocity, appropriate activity and intimate intersubjectivity of the psychotherapy/counseling attending relationship/process; such that essential, necessary and appropriate actions and interactions naturally flow and organically follow from the clear and open awarenesses of, and the deep and full connections between, psychotherapists/counselors and human beings.[12]

Sacred and wise human living are the attentive experiencing of self-awakening, transforming and developing that is equivalent to the journeying of our Human Souls from ego-identifying with body, mind, others and the world to Self-identifying with Spirit, Psyche/Consciousness, fellow Human Beings and the Multiverse; the wayfaring from the '10,000 things' to Tao. Psychotherapy is one beneficial way of attending to, encouraging, supporting, assisting, facilitating and guiding at least some part of the natural unfolding of the wayfaring journey returning us Home to our Selves, Souls and Spirit.

Rendition

The present work, titled '*Tao Virtuosity Experience*', technically is not a translation of the *Tao Te Ching* text. Rather, it is a rendition and, more precisely, the literary equivalent of a jazz rendition characterized by some occasional solo improvised departures from an originally arranged composition.

This rendition, the synopses and commentaries are based upon: 1) studying, correlating, cross-referencing and meditating upon over one-hundred English language translations, versions, interpretations, variations and adaptations of the text and four bilingual texts; 2) consulting Chinese language dictionaries to define the etymological radicals and phonetics and extended meanings of each one of the approximately eight-hundred different Chinese characters comprising the approximately five-thousand two-hundred total number of characters of the text; 3) reading numerous relevant materials of Chinese Taoist philosophical schools/Tao Chia and religious sects/Tao Chiao; 4) practicing with several Taoist Masters; 5) educating, training, supervising and mentoring counseling and clinical psychology graduate students and 4) conducting psychotherapy and counseling in a wide variety of inpatient and outpatient clinical treatment facilities and group and individual private practice settings.

This rendition is not intended to be about Taoism as 1) formulating a way of psychotherapy involving particular theoretical concepts and methodological techniques for use in treating specific clinical conditions or patient populations and 2) contributing yet another 'ism-ology' to the field of psychotherapy. At the very most, the present work may be considered to be a westernized urban neo-Taoist way of understanding and conducting any psychotherapy practice that integrates Eastern psychospiritual and Western psychotherapeutic personal and transpersonal attitudes and approaches, regardless of particular theoretical orientations or methodological applications.

Also, this rendition is not an owner's operational 'how to do' manual for psychotherapy practice since, in general, it does not include concrete and detailed examples of specific interpretations, interactions and interventions in the attending relationship/process. The greatest emphasis of psychotherapeutic agency, potency, efficacy and intimacy is upon the natural, integral and practical modes, states and qualities of the Tao-identified being, awakened consciousness, clear awareness, full attention and deep connection of true attenders rather than upon any particular kinds of theoretical conceptions entertained, interpersonal relationships engaged in or methodological procedures utilized, e.g.,

Te/Virtuosity

❖ mode of attending/attention *to*/heeding of phenomena.

❖ state of nondual awakeness/awareness/accepting/acknowledging.

❖ state of letting-be/individuality/uniqueness/integrity/receiving.

❖ mode of 'knowing'/clearness/consciousness/openness of mind.

❖ qualities of non-externalizing/abstracting/objectifying.

❖ qualities of non-presupposing/preconceiving/predefining.

❖ qualities of non-portending/interrogating/interdicting/interjecting.

❖ quality of intersubjective interpreting/interpretations.

Yin/Yang Ch'i

❖ mode of attending/attentive *to*/caring for needs.

❖ state of empathic attuning/adjusting/aligning/according.

❖ state of letting-go/alternating/balancing/voiding/reversing.

❖ mode of 'having'/emptiness/centeredness/equalness of heart.

❖ qualities of non-assessing/evaluating/desiring.

❖ qualities of non-prejudging/preferring/pre-empting.

❖ qualities of non-extending/interpolating/interposing/ interceding.

❖ quality of interdependent interchanging/interchanges.

WU WEI CH'I

❖ mode of attending/attending *to*/taking care of business.

❖ state of synergic entraining/acceding/allowing/accompanying.

❖ state of going-with/sourcing/yielding/following/returning.

❖ mode of 'doing'/stillness/cooperativeness/calmness of will.

❖ qualities of non-controlling/manipulating/forcing.

❖ qualities of non-preplanning/predetermining/prefabricating.

❖ qualities of non-intending/interfering/interrupting/ intercepting.

❖ quality of interactive intervening/interventions.

TAO/ULTIMACY

❖ mode of attending/attendance *at*/participating in events.

❖ state of co-existing beingness/affiliating/allying/abiding.

❖ state of being-with/joining/communing/uniting/residing.

❖ mode of 'being'/oneness/connectedness/wholeness of being.

❖ qualities of non-separating/alienating/fragmenting.

❖ qualities of non-precedence/pre-eminence/precluding.

❖ qualities of non-pretending/intermixing/interlocking/ interfusing.

❖ quality of interrelated interconnecting/interconnections.

Rather, this rendition, the synopses and commentaries are purely and simply an opportunity to express some of whatever observations, discoveries and connections have been made during sixty two years of integrating the psychospiritual and psychotherapeutic attitudes and approaches of the disciplines of ancient Chinese Taoism and modern Western Psychology.

The passages, synopses and commentaries of the rendition are best read with slow, deep and full breathing in a state of quiet relaxation and open awareness, i.e., with a relatively clear mind, empty heart, still will and free Spirit, so as to allow their meanings to resonate more deeply and fully in your unique inner being and for your unique journeying and intimate wayfaring along the wilderness pathways, flowing watercourses and awaiting frontiers of Tao.

If the following material is in some, or any, way of interest, value, encouragement, support, assistance, guidance, use and/or benefit to you in awakening, discovering, experiencing, understanding and sharing your precious human being, conscious human living and unique wayfaring journeying; I am infinitely pleased and eternally grateful.

Raymond Bart Vespe
Santa Rosa, California
Vernal Equinox 2016

TAO

ROAD/PATH/WAY
PRINCIPLE/DOCTRINE
REALITY/LOGOS/TRUTH
LAW/ORDER/METHOD
SPEAK/LEAD/GUIDE
THE WAY

MAKING STEP BY STEP HEADWAY ON THE WAY ONE
IS VISIONING AND PROCEEDING

ABSOLUTE/ESSENTIAL/ONE/ULTIMATE REALITY
CONSTANT/REGULAR/INFINITE/ETERNAL
ORIGIN/SOURCE/DESTINY/FINALITY
TRANSCENDENT/NO-THING/NON-BEING
IMMANENT/ALL THINGS/ALL-BEING
NATURE/HEAVEN-EARTH/UNIVERSE
ALL THAT IS/AS IT IS / EVERYWHERE
AT ONCE/HERE-NOW

Experience 1

Mystery and Marvels

Tao being tao-ed is the counterpart of Constant Tao[13]
Names being named are counterparts
of its Constant Name

Unnamable Non-Being is preceding Heaven-Earth
Named Being is Mother of all beings

Being thought-free is glimpsing eternal Mystery
Being thought-full is beholding infinite Miracles[14]

Mystery and Miracles are one and the same
And are only being named differently

This identity is Ultimate Mystery[15]
Most dark, most deep, Mystery upon Mystery
Gateway of all Wondrous Marvels[16]

Synopsis 1 ❖ Mystery and Marvels

Tao, as the Supreme Ultimate Reality, is both transcendent and non-objectifiable and immanent and objectifiable. The deep and dark transcendent Non-Being and Mystery of Tao's originating are being glimpsed when the mind is in its non-phenomenal world clear and free of desire-based conceptualizing activities. The structured and boundaried immanent being and Miracles of Tao's forming are being beheld when the mind is in its phenomenal world bound and limited by desire-based conceptualizing operations. Miracles are hidden within the inner absence of Mystery and Mystery is revealed in the outer presencing of Miracles. Mystery and Miracles are one identity which is a gateway for experiencing all of the Wondrous Marvels of Tao's manifesting in conscious experience.

Commentary 1 ❖ Mystery and Marvels

Wise attenders are:

Not obscuring and reducing the quintessential reality and absolutely unique identities of human beings by only abstracting and objectifying (making the real unreal) them as patients/counselees and by only reifying and defining (making the unreal real) them through diagnostic labeling and case formulating.

Regarding the open matrix of Tao, the alternating dynamics of Yin Ch'i/Yang Ch'i energies and the flowing kinetics of Wu Wei Ch'i activities as the ultimate context, frame, crucible, container, center, ground and locus of control of the attending relationship/process.

Regarding human being, living, growing, transforming and awakening as an awesome Mystery of origination, a precious Miracle of formation, a wondrous Marvel of manifestation and a joyful Magnificence of completion to be honored, respected, witnessed, treasured, nourished, celebrated and shared.[17/18]

EXPERIENCE 2

INTERDEPENDENT COMPLEMENTARITY

As people, when we are conceiving beauty
We are simultaneously invoking non-beauty
As people, when we are conceiving good
We are simultaneously invoking non-good

Being and Non-Being are co-creating each other
Difficult and easy are contrasting each other
Long and short are comparing each other
High and low are complementing each other
Music and voice are composing each other
Before and after are completing each other

As wise human beings, we are:
Influencing activities without doing any 'thing'
Revealing learnings without teaching any 'thing'

As wise human beings, we are:
Attending whatever is happening
Supporting without possessing
Assisting without controlling
Accomplishing without crediting

As wise human beings
We are not requiring gratitude
Work is being completed and forgotten

SYNOPSIS 2 ❖ INTERDEPENDENT COMPLEMENTARITY

All human awarenesses, relationships, activities and experiencing, when conceptualized and named, i.e., discriminated, defined, evaluated and judged, are simultaneously bipolar in nature. The many and varied experiential phenomena are not mutually exclusive dualistic opposites but, rather, are interdependent and reciprocal complements. Wise human beings are identifying *as* Tao and are not intentionally teaching any 'thing' nor purposely 'doing' any 'thing', yet the living reality and truth of their presence, like other natural phenomena, are in-fluencing (creating an in-flowing) activities and revealing learnings. Wise human beings are attending, supporting, assisting and contributing to completing human beings and surrounding circumstances without possessing, controlling, needing credit or gratitude. They simply are being who they are, doing what they do and forgetting about it.

COMMENTARY 2 ❖ INTERDEPENDENT COMPLEMENTARITY

Wise attenders are:

Understanding the experiences and concerns of human beings in a complementary bipolar and reciprocally interdependent manner and are not exclusively making one-sided dualistic interpretations and unilateral interventions.[19]

Understanding that when pathology, illness, maladjustment and conflict are being conceived; health, wellness, adjustment and harmony are simultaneously being invoked and that:

Conscious and unconscious are co-creating each other

Resistance and collaboration are contrasting each other

Chronic and acute are comparing each other

Elation and depression are complementing each other

Nonverbal and verbal are composing each other

History and termination are completing each other

Aware of the influential educative and transformative power of presence in the attending relationship/process and are allowing it to naturally proceed and spontaneously unfold through non-judgmental accepting, non-possessive supporting, non-controlling assisting and non-attached completing without intruding, interpreting or interfering.

EXPERIENCE 3

CONCEPTLESS AND DESIRELESS

As people, when we are:
Not exalting developed human beings
We are not competing
Not treasuring rare objects
We are not stealing
Not displaying desirable goods
Our heart-minds are not longing

As wise human beings,
When we are governing
Heart-minds are emptying
Belly centers are filling
Ambitious wills are weakening
Supporting bones are strengthening

As wise human beings,
We are guiding people
To be conceptless and desireless
And cleverness and craftiness
To be ineffective

By practicing non-interfering
This State is self-regulating

SYNOPSIS 3 ❖ CONCEPTLESS AND DESIRELESS

Exalting others, desiring things and displaying goods are promoting imitating and competing, pursuing and acquiring and envying and longing. Wise human beings are modeling and assisting people in developing a deeper, fuller and stronger focus, structure and support for their inner core selves. Without interfering in the lives of people, they are guiding them to become free of such concepts of, and desires for, externalized others, objects and things and to be valuing and living their true and unique selves, to be self-correcting and self-regulating and to be achieving a state of safety, stability, security and sufficiency.

COMMENTARY 3 ❖ CONCEPTLESS AND DESIRELESS

Wise attenders are:

Not overvaluing and emulating master psychotherapists/counselors and not treasuring and appropriating preferred theories and techniques or parading and promoting desirable outcomes, e.g., particular rational insights, emotional releases, behavioral changes, conflict resolutions, psychic openings, Spiritual awakenings or other treatment agendas.

Assisting human beings in clearing their minds of obsessive thinking, emptying their hearts of possessive feeling and stilling their wills of compulsive behaving and are facilitating an opening to deeper instinctual experiencing and inner Spiritual strengthening of their core selves.

Not using clever interpretations, cunning interactions or crafty interventions in the attending relationship/process that would be interfering with human beings' self-awareness, self-experiencing, self-understanding, self-accepting and self-regulating.

EXPERIENCE 4

INEXHAUSTIBLE HARMONIZING

Tao is a state of empty harmony
Using it is never exhausting it
It is this deep and vast
Unfathomable Source of all beings

It is:
Smoothing our sharp edges
Loosening our tight knots
Softening our bright lights
Settling our dusty worlds

Deep, still, pure, clear
It is remaining forever

Its origin is unknown
It is existing before all beginnings
Before a Supreme Creator/Creatrix

Synopsis 4 ❖ Inexhaustible Harmonizing

The Tao-State is being one of perfect dynamic balance, an empty harmony, formless field and open ground devoid of experiential contents and objects. But Tao's empty harmony is the pure potential of the plenum void, always at its maximum potential for originating and presencing forms. As such, it is the deep, vast, unfathomable and inexhaustible root-source and open matrix of all created, forming and manifesting phenomena. Through the bipolar interactive dynamics of Yin Ch'i/Yang Ch'i energies, Original Tao is constantly, continually and continuously alternating, counterbalancing, equalizing, centralizing, harmonizing, voiding and reversing manifest forms so that their extremes are naturally and automatically compensated for, revert to their complements and maintain a steady state of dynamic equilibrium, e.g., sharpness is smoothed, tightness is loosened, brightness is softened and dustiness is settled. The Tao-State; deep, clear, still and pure; is beyond beginnings and endings, a Supreme Creator/Creatrix and human beings.

Commentary 4 ❖ Inexhaustible Harmonizing

Wise attenders are:

Being clear of preferred conceptual formulations and theories, empty of particular emotional investments and attachments and still of typical behavioral purposes and interventions and are identifying *as* the open matrix of Tao which is originating, forming, manifesting and completing all of the myriad variety of experiences in the attending relationship/process.

Allowing the attending relationship/process to proceed and unfold naturally, organically and spontaneously and to be automatically self-adjusting, compensating, equalizing, centralizing and harmonizing through the interactive bipolar dynamics of Yin Ch'i/Yang Ch'i energies. Rough spots are naturally smoothed out, tight places are naturally loosened up, hard times are naturally softened and unclear issues are naturally settled.

Identifying *as* the deepness, clearness, stillness and oneness of Original Tao prior to the presenting issues, past histories and symptomatic etiologies of human beings and are getting out of the way and letting Tao operate through the alternating dynamics of Yin Ch'i/Yang Ch'i energy and the flowing kinetics of Wu Wei Ch'i activity.

Experience 5

Empty Center

Heaven-Earth is being impartial
By regarding all beings as sacrificial offerings
As wise human beings, we are being impartial
By regarding all people as sacrificial offerings

Heaven-Earth's centerspace
Is being like a bellows
Empty and inexhaustible
The more it is pumping
The more it is generating

Many words are displacing emptiness
Most developed is identifying as
The empty inner Center

Synopsis 5 ❖ Empty Center

Tao, as Heaven-Earth, is being indifferent and impartial toward the existing of human beings; as are natural phenomena such as sunrises, rainstorms, forest fires and tidal waves. The cyclical process of birthing, growing, developing, declining and dying is going on naturally and independently. Each being is only a small part of an overall process, a minute speck in a vast ground of being, a tiny arc in a great orbit of changing and, as such, is an offering of sacrifice (holy-making) to the entire whole of living. The reality of living is ephemeral with all beings coming quickly, staying briefly and passing quickly. Wise human beings are regarding all human beings compassionately and impartially as precious transient incarnations of a great universal holy-making. The open matrix and empty center of Tao is constantly, continually and continuously moving and inexhaustibly generating phenomena as the dynamic alternating of Yin Ch'i/Yang Ch'i energies like the rhythmic contracting and expanding of the systolic/diastolic pulsing of the heart and the inspiration/expiration of the breath. Wise human beings are identifying *as* the empty inner center of the plenum void, the originating matrix and open Heart of Tao, and are not filling and displacing its emptiness and openness with too many words.

Commentary 5 ❖ Empty Center

Wise attenders are:

Identifying *as* the empty center of perfectly balanced Tao and are receiving, reflecting and responding to human beings with impartiality and equality, but not indifference or impersonality; by attentive listening, deeper nonverbal connection and the power of relative silence.

Compassionately regarding human beings as Sacred, precious, unique and transient incarnations and personifications of the great universal holy-making of the Mystery, Miracles, Marvels and Magnificence of human being and living. The universe of Tao is the One-turning and our individual life is the blessed gift of our one-turn.

Using few verbalizations that are displacing their identifying *as* the empty and open inner center; the Heart, Axis and Pivot of Tao; and its inexhaustible generating and manifesting of all of the myriad phenomena of the attending relationship/process.

EXPERIENCE 6

VALLEY SPIRIT

Valley Spirit is never dying out
She is subtly and profoundly Feminine

The gateway of this Mysterious Feminine
Is the Root-Source of Heaven-Earth

She is everpresencing and everlasting
Utilizing Her is never wearing out

SYNOPSIS 6 ❖ VALLEY SPIRIT

Tao as open matrix, empty center, plenum void and root-source is the quintessential Feminine deep Spirit and creative power of the fertile valley. As Creatrix, She is perpetually and inexhaustibly Mysteriously originating, Miraculously forming, Marvelously manifesting and Magnificently completing all forms, beings and phenomena of life. She is the primordial and original Great Mother; dark, mysterious, profound and subtle. From Her deep womb, the gateway of all life, are coming Heaven-Earth, the totality of all beings and their natural organic living processes. She is nourishing longevity, inexhaustibility and immortality in the everpresencing and everlasting timeless moment of the eternal now, beyond living and dying.

COMMENTARY 6 ❖ VALLEY SPIRIT

Wise attenders are:

Identifying *as* the Valley Spirit, the Feminine Spirit of the open, deep, rich and fertile valley in its mystery, profundity, subtlety and eternity and with the Tao-State of being all-creating, all-nourishing, all-sustaining, all-receiving and all-fulfilling.

Being-like the Feminine Valley Spirit in their inner depth and central core and are tapping into the creative root-source and inexhaustible re-source of their Heavenly-Earthly Tao-nature, the gateway of the natural unfolding of the attending relationship/process.

Living *as* the abiding Spirit of the fecund valley and connecting with the wellsprings and fountainheads of the constant presencing and endless flowing of each and every attending experience by drawing from the inexhaustible reservoir and reserves of the awesome power of the maternal feminine, are never burning-out and are constantly being replenished, restored and renewed.

EXPERIENCE 7

EMBODYING NO-SELF

Heaven-Earth is everlasting
Timeless and eternal
By not generating itself
By not living for itself

As wise human beings, we are:
Being absent and constantly presencing
Being behind and constantly advancing
As wise human beings, we are:
Having no self-interests
Embodying Universal Self

SYNOPSIS 7 ❖ EMBODYING NO-SELF

Tao, as Heaven-Earth, is timeless and eternal because it is unborn and undying, a nondual totality and not a separated and divided object subject to conditions and limitations. As such, Tao is nonpersonal/transpersonal and not objectifiably self-reflexive, i.e., without being-in-itself or being-for-itself. It is, purely and simply Being-*As*-Itself. Wise human beings are similarly undivided and are embodying the essential and universal reality of Tao *as* their innermost, deepest, centermost, truest and utmost nature or Virtuosity/Te. Being absent, i.e., relatively anonymous and free of ego-identity, and being behind, i.e., relatively unpretentious and free of ego-precedence; wise human beings are having no self-interest but, rather No-Self interest, are not invested in nor attached to a separate ego-image or self-concept and are embodying and personifying the Universal Self as they are presencing and developing.[20]

COMMENTARY 7 ❖ EMBODYING NO-SELF

Wise attenders are:

Identifying *as* their timeless Heavenly-Earthly Tao-nature and No-Self and are not having any self-interests in, egotistical investments in, nor personal attachments to, the realities, truths and actualities of the attending relationship/process.

Being relatively egoless, selfless and anonymous; free of personal ego-images, social facades and professional personas and are embodying, personifying, reflecting, identifying as and empathizing with the Universal Self of human beings.

Being low-profile and low-impact minimalists who are stepping back, staying behind and getting out of the way and are allowing space for human beings to be at the unique forefront of their self-presencing, self-experiencing, self-developing and self-owning.

EXPERIENCE 8

BEING WATER-LIKE

Most developed goodness is being like water
Water is benefiting all beings without contending

Water is dwelling in depths ignored by people
And, so, is approximating Tao

As water-like goodness, we are loving:
Earthiness in dwelling
Deepness in heart-mind
Naturalness in relating
Truthfulness in speaking
Orderliness in governing
Effectiveness in serving
Timeliness in activities

As wise water-like human beings
We are not contending
And there is no harming

SYNOPSIS 8 ❖ BEING WATER-LIKE

Tao, as water, is a standard and model wise human beings are internalizing, assimilating, embodying, personifying, enacting and identifying *as*. The life-nourishing goodness and life-sustaining benefit of water are naturally flowing into and dwelling in low and deep places. Water is flowing around, under and over solid objects without resisting, competing, contending or conflicting. Water is yielding and changing to adapt, accomodate, comply, conform and accord naturally. Water is Tao-like and the process of living is flowing along like waterways and watercourses that are making and finding their ways upon, within, beneath and through the Earth. The goodness and benefit of wise human beings are water-like, being close to the Earth, deep, natural, true, orderly, effective and timely. Wise human beings, *as* water-like, are being modest and humble, are not contending with any beings and are benefiting all beings without harming any.

COMMENTARY 8 ❖ BEING WATER-LIKE

Wise attenders are:

Identifying *as* the water-like nature and goodness of Tao; being fresh, flowing, vitalizing, nourishing and sustaining without rigid rules, fixed roles and stale rituals and are flexibly adapting to the fluid and everchanging valences, vectors, contours, trajectories and coursings of the lives of unique human beings and the novel flowingness, ongoingness and unfolding of the attending relationship/process.

Loving:

Solid grounding in concrete, direct and immediate experiencing.

Deep inner heart-to-heart emotional contact and connection.

Open, honest, true, genuine and authentic human relationships.

Sharing the reality, truth, beauty and grace of inner experiencing.

Naturally balancing, self-regulating and harmonizing .

Effectively making meaningful differences to human beings.

Attuning to and according with rhythms in human activities.

Moving and following along, naturally, appropriately, cooperatively and collaboratively with the attending relationship/process and the actionless activity of Wu Wei Ch'i flowing kinetics as they are drawn by gravity downstream; not resisting resistance; not competing, conflicting or contending with human beings and not engaging in power struggles; to the lower, deeper and Earthly nature of Tao, benefiting all human beings without harming or rewounding any.

EXPERIENCE 9

STOPPING IN TIME

Filling to the point of overflowing
Is not as developed as stopping in time
And conserving an empty space

Honing to the point of oversharpening
Is not as developed as stopping in time
And preserving a solid edge

When jade and gold are filling our houses
We are needing to safeguard them
Taking pride in wealth and fame
Is bringing downfall and collapse

Withdrawing when work is completed
Such is Heaven's Tao

Synopsis 9 ❖ Stopping in Time

Not stopping in time is overdoing that is exceeding capacity and limits by either adding or taking away too much. When too much is put in or added to an empty space, it is being overfilled and overloaded, its capacty is being exceeded and lost and there is no available space for anything to enter. When too much is being taken away or subtracted from a solid form, it is being overthinned and weakened, its limit is being exceeded and lost and there is no substantial edge for anything to meet. Too full, e.g., wealth, is being closed and heavy and too sharp, e.g., fame, is being thin and weak, which are leading to downfall and collapse. Wise human beings, embodying Heaven's Tao, are not overdoing by adding or subtracting too much, are completing work, stopping in time and withdrawing. They are not needing to protect themselves from spilling, breaking or losing either empty and open space or solid and keen edge or anything else that was not needing to be had or done in the first place.

Commentary 9 ❖ Stopping in Time

Wise attenders are:

Using succinct additive and pointed refining statements that are filling in and amplifying and honing down and sharpening the attending relationship/process without overdoing; making extensive assessments, extraneous reflections, elaborate interpretations, extended monologues, prolonged interactions and excessive interventions that are unecessary, irrelevant, inefficient, ineffective and wasteful.

Conserving empty open spaces and preserving full solid edges by stopping in time when an appropriate limit is reached or a sufficient point is made in reflections, feedback and dialogues or in processes, exercises and experiments.

Not amassing a wealthy storehouse of response repertoires, treatment strategies and formulaic procedures and not priding in professional status, famous reputations or lucrative practices; which ultimately are only bringing about empathic failures, derailing of the attending relationship/process and its eventual untimely termination.

Rather, purely and simply allowing the work of attending at/in/to the relationship/process to naturally complete itself, and are humbly and modestly stopping in time and stepping back, content in the perfect adequacy and sufficiency of the present moment just *as* it is.

TE

VIRTUE
POWER/ENERGY
CHARACTER/EXCELLENCE
RIGHTEOUSNESS
GOODNESS/KINDNESS

LISTENING/UNDERSTANDING/RELATING
UPRIGHTLY/STRAIGHTFORWARDLY FROM
THE REALITY/TRUTH OF ONE'S HEART-MIND.

INBORN/INNATE TAO-NATURE
UNIQUE INDIVIDUALITY
INNER TRUTH/INTEGRITY
EFFICACIOUS POTENCY
PRESENCE/IN-FLUENCE
VIRTUOSITY/GENIUS

EXPERIENCE 10

EMBODYING VIRTUOSITY

As wise human beings, we are:
Unifying our Heavenly-Earthly Souls
And embodying undivided Oneness
Conserving our vital energies
And embodying infant suppleness
Purifying our inner vision
And embodying perfect clearness

As wise human beings, we are:
Loving people and governing this State
Without knowing or doing anything unnatural

As wise human beings, we are:
Embodying maternal nature
Opening and closing Heaven's gateways
Illuminating interior dimensions
Without taking interfering actions

Synopsis 10 ❖ Embodying Virtuosity

Wise human beings are unifying Heavenly and Earthly Souls, conserving vital energy, purifying inner vision and self-regulating naturally. They are embodying nondual unity, infant flexibility, intuitive clarity, human intimacy and spontaneous harmony without intellectualizing and manipulating. Wise human beings are embodying maternity by being receptive, reflective and responsive rather than resistive, retentive and reactive. They are awakened, attentive and attuned to inner experiencing and are not taking intrusive, invasive or interfering actions. Wise human beings are contributing to bringing forth, nourishing, supporting, assisting and developing human beings without being possessive, controlling or forcing. As such, they are embodying and enacting the mysterious creativity and originality and the miraculous potency and efficacy of Tao and Virtuosity/Te.

Commentary 10 ❖ Embodying Virtuosity

Wise attenders are:

Unifying their physical and Spiritual being, embodying undivided oneness, conserving life energies and refining intuitive abilities and are deeply appreciating human beings, making harmonious interactions, clear interpretations and flexible interventions in the attending relationship/process without unnaturally confronting, intellectualizing or manipulating.

Identifying *as* their feminine maternal nature and are acknowledging, accepting and receiving (letting-be); attuning, according and reflecting (letting-go); allowing, accompanying and responding (going-with) and affiliating, allying and residing (being-with) in the attending relationship/process without making unnatural intrusive, invasive or interfering interactions and interventions.

Validating, nourishing, supporting, assisting and contributing to the developing of human beings in the attending relationship/process without attaching to them, controlling interactions, forcing change or investing in outcomes. They, purely and simply, are *being* their Tao-nature/Virtuosity/Te, their 'Great technical skill in the practice of a fine art'.

Experience 11

Usefulness of Emptiness

Thirty spokes are radiating from one unifying hub
A wheel's usefulness is its empty centerspace

Clay is being shaped, forming a vessel
A vessel's usefulness is its empty innerspace

Doors and windows are being cut out, making a room
A room's usefulness is its empty openspace

Benefit is obtaining
From the being of solid outer form

Utility is obtaining
From the Non-Being of empty inner space

Synopsis 11 ❖ Usefulness of Emptiness

Most objects, things and beings are having an external or peripheral surface form and an internal or central depth space. While the being and presence of the outer form are providing a substantial or full surrounding and containing structure that is of necessary benefit; it is the Non-Being and absence of the inner space that are providing an insubstantial or empty inner and available space that is of essential use. Functionality and utility are requiring an optimally balanced interrelationship of solid form and empty space. This empty inner centerspace is an openness whereby the creative potential and capacity for generation, formation and manifestation are at their maximum. This is the open matrix, deep womb, formless field and plenum void, the abode and Heart of Tao. While benefit is deriving from solid outer form, it is the spacious inner emptiness that is creating and enabling usefulness.[21]

Commentary 11 ❖ Usefulness of Emptiness

Wise attenders are:

Identifying *as* the empty and open inner centerspace of Tao as the most useful and beneficial way of being in the attending relationship/process when integrated and balanced with contextual structure, holding environments, containing frames, definite boundaries, consistent limits and solid connecting relationships.

Flexibly balancing and rhythmically integrating both the benefits of solid structure and clear form and the usefulness of open structure and free form in the spontaneity of their reflections, interpretations, interactions and interventions.

Experiencing the value of, and necessity for, silences, pauses, rests, intervals and gaps in the ongoingness of the attending relationship/process in order to allow inner contact, reflections and connections; to source, follow and complete behaviors; to absorb, assimilate and integrate awarenesses, feelings and insights and to focus, deepen and appreciate experiences.

EXPERIENCE 12

INNER EXPERIENCING

As people:
Many colors are blinding our eyes
Many sounds are deafening our ears
Many tastes are numbing our palates

Hunting and chasing are crazing our heart-minds
Getting and keeping are impeding our developing

As wise human beings, we are:
Attending to belly not eyes
Rejecting the outer 'that'
Accepting the inner 'This'

Synopsis 12 ❖ Inner Experiencing

Intense and excessive sensory stimulation are overloading, overwhelming and deadening our sense organs. Frantically seeking and pursuing exciting experiences in the outer world of sensory stimulation are crazing our minds and hearts and acquiring and hoarding are impeding our maturing and developing. Engaging in, or vicariously experiencing, the thrilling distractions and diversions of extreme entertainment, sport and amusement are only providing a temporary fix for addictions that must be constantly fed and continually re-fed. Wise human beings are rejecting excitedly eyeing stimulating activities in the outer world of appearances and attractions and, instead, are enthusiastically cultivating a deeper, organismic and fulfilling inner presence of Tao. Rather than compulsively seeking repeated stimulation, activation and intensification of end-states of sensory arousal; wise human beings are freely welcoming re-creating, potentiating and actualizing Tao-States of Spiritual awakening.

Commentary 12 ❖ Inner Experiencing

Wise attenders are:

Experiencing that too much sensory stimulation and intensity are causing the body to close up, shut down or turn off and are not engaging in flashy reflections, brilliant interpretations, stellar interactions or dazzling interventions in the attending relationship/process that only intimidate and overwhelm human beings; creating muscular contractions and armoring, energetic constriction and blocks, cognitive defenses and emotional resistance and interpersonal inhibition, distancing and withdrawal.

Avoiding repeating sensory-based, stimulation-driven, arousal-seeking and excitation-promoting behaviors and activities in the attending relationship/process by using soft voices, slow movements, calm gestures and gentle responses that naturally soften, melt, release and open defenses and resistances from inside out.

Assisting human beings in transforming obsessively desiring, compulsively pursuing and addictively engaging in overly stimulating, intense and exciting end-states of sensory arousal 'out there' in the external world of objects, relationships and activities and, rather, are encouraging, supporting, assisting and facilitating their contact and connection with deeper, instinctual and organismic 'in here' core Self-experiences.

EXPERIENCE 13

NO-SELF, NO TROUBLE

Be fearing favor like fearing disgrace
Be regarding our selves as great trouble

What is meant by:
Fearing favor like fearing disgrace?
Favor is dishonoring and demeaning
We are afraid of losing it
We are afraid of having it
This is why favor, like disgrace,
Is frightening

What is meant by:
Regarding ourselves as great trouble?
We are having great trouble
Because we are having a 'self'
If we are having No-Self
We are having no trouble

Valuing all beings as our true selves
We can be trusted by all beings
Loving all beings as our true selves
We can be entrusted with all beings.

SYNOPSIS 13 ❖ NO-SELF, NO TROUBLE

While there is an apparent difference between favor and disgrace, they both are two yin-yang sides of the same one bipolar coin of Tao and disgrace is hidden within favor. Favor and disgrace are both dishonoring and demeaning in relation to the natural worth and dignity of human beings. Because we have an objectified image and concept of ourselves (an ego),[22] we are having trouble. Otherwise, there would only be an experience of ourselves as whole, without a subject-object or noun-verb division. Being a non-objectified Self or No-Self is being Tao-like, i.e., a nondual unity and identity without subject-object distinction or where subject and object are in perfect balance. This Tao-State of No-Self eliminates the trouble inhering in subject-object and self-other dualistic objectifications and distinctions. Valuing and loving human beings as non-objectified No-Selves, we can be their trustworthy and trusted guardians, custodians, caregivers and stewards.

COMMENTARY 13 ❖ NO-SELF, NO TROUBLE

Wise attenders are:

Not favoring only certain human beings, not using only favorite theories and techniques, not offering only favorable feedback, not making only favorable interactions and interventions, and not achieving only favorable progress and outcomes or attaining only a favorable professional practice or reputation.

Not identifying with, being invested in or attached to or positively reinforcing ego-identities, self-images, self-concepts, false self-identities, personal facades and professional personas, transference and countertransference projections and projective identifications and are not experiencing their inherent troubles.

Relating to human beings with impartiality and equality and are deeply honoring, valuing and respecting them as their own real, true, genuine and authentic selves and, therefore, are able to be trusted by and entrusted with them.

EXPERIENCE 14

TAPESTRY OF TAO

Looking for it, we are not seeing it
It is invisible, colorless
Listening for it, we are not hearing it
It is inaudible, soundless
Reaching for it, we are not touching it
It is intangible, formless

These three are beyond our experiencing
And are merging into Oneness

Its height is not light
Its depth is not dark
Continuously, endlessly
The Unnamable is cycling on
Returning to No-Thingness

It is this formless form, imageless image
Abstruse, obscure, subtle, elusive
Confronting it, we are seeing no beginning
Following it, we are seeing no ending

We are internalizing ancient Tao
Regulating present circumstances
Embodying primordial originating
This tapestry of Tao

Synopsis 14 ❖ Tapestry of Tao

Tao is a transphenomenal, suprasensory, non-objectifiable and ineffable unity. It is n-dimensional and multidimensional, beyond the linear dimensions of space-time and before all beginnings and after all endings. Tao moves cyclically from originating, forming, presencing and completing individualized forms to reverting and returning to Non-Being, No-Thingness, formlessness and absence. It is hidden, indistinct, ephemeral, evanescent, elusive and evasive and can only be subtly sensed internally, intuitively, indirectly and insubstantially in suggestive hints, faint traces and fleeting glimpses. Embodying, internalizing and identifying *as* Tao are allowing us to be originating and regulating present circumstances; to be living more truly, fully and harmoniously in the present moment and to be contributing our unique individual threads to the long lineage of weavers of the rich and beautiful tapestry of Tao.

Commentary 14 ❖ Tapestry of Tao

Wise attenders are:

Identifying *as* their innermost, deepest, centermost, truest and utmost Tao-nature which essentially is transphenomenal, numinous and noumenal and beyond experiencing but which is being subtly and intuitively accessed through meditative practices of visualization, concentration, reflection, contemplation and absorption and is embodied as their Virtuosity/Te.

Experiencing that, while Tao is beyond the space-time dimensions and limitations of ordinary human consciousness, it is the 'locus of agency and control' for naturally originating, organizing and regulating the many and varied phenomena occurring in the attending relationship/process.

Identifying *as* the nonmaterial and formless reality of primordial and original Tao; and are embodying, internalizing and assimilating its Non-Beingness that is generating, forming, manifesting, completing and harmoniously interweaving the richly textured and vibrantly colored tapestry of ongoing human experiencing throughout the life-course of the attending relationship/process.

EXPERIENCE 15

ANCIENT TAO-MASTERS

As ancient Tao-Masters, we are:
Subtly mysterious, profoundly identified
Too deep to be experienced
Beyond ordinary understanding
Only described approximately

We are being:
Careful, as crossing frozen streams
Watchful, as attending to all sides
Respectful, as visiting guests
Yielding, as melting ice
Natural, as unhewn wood
Open, as spacious valleys
Undifferentiated, as muddy waters

We are purifying muddy waters through serenity
We are vivifying still waters through activity

We are embodying Tao
And not filling to overflowing
Not overflowing
There is no spilling and refilling

Synopsis 15 ❖ Ancient Tao-Masters

Wise human beings, like ancient Tao-Masters, are embodying, internalizing, assimilating, personifying and profoundly identifying *as* the mysterious transphenomenality of Tao. They are being careful, circumspect, respectful, yielding, natural, open and merged. The reality and potency of their energetic presence are naturally and spontaneously balancing, centralizing and harmonizing the extremes of bipolar experiencing. Wise human beings, like Tao-Masters, are being grounded and centered in the sufficiency of the rhythmically alternating Yin Ch'i/Yang Ch'i of filling and emptying and the sequentially flowing Wu Wei Ch'i of coming and going of life experiences and are balancing the clarity of stillness and the vivacity of flowingness. They are being adequately and sufficiently fulfilled by reality just as it is without needing to add anything to it or subtract anything from it or to undo or redo the already done or overdone.

Commentary 15 ❖ Ancient Tao-Masters

Wise attenders are:

Identifying *as* their intuitive sensing of the mystery, profundity and subtlety of their Tao-nature rather than with ordinary rational, conceptual and intellectual ways of understanding themselves.

Like human beings wayfaring through stages of:

Carefully beginning a great psychotherapeutic life passage.

Circumspect with a global awareness of all beings and living.

Respectfully acknowledging the host, gift and heart of living.

Yielding and flowing with whatever is happening in living.

Identifying as the primordial origin and simplicity of living.

Openly centered in the deep ground and vast space of living.

Equally including, accepting and merging with all living beings.

Experiencing that the efficacious power of their presence alone is clarifying confusion through their serenity and is enlivening stuckness through their fluidity and is naturally in-fluencing the compensatory self-correcting, counterbalancing and harmonizing of other bipolar experiences.

Making simple, succinct, economical, timely and efficient interventions in the attending relationship/process without any overdoing that is necessitating undoing or re-doing them.

EXPERIENCE 16

RETURNING TO TAO

Attaining complete emptiness
Maintaining constant stillness
We are witnessing all beings
Coming into being and cyclically returning
All beings are flourishing in living
Each one returning to Root-Source

Returning to Root-Source is tranquility
Tranquility is returning to original nature
Returning to originality is eternal constancy

Embodying constancy is being illuminated
Ignoring constancy is inviting disaster

Embodying constancy is being all-embracing
Being all-embracing is being impartial
Being impartial is being universal
Being universal is being natural
Being natural is being in accord with Tao
According with Tao is being everlasting
Free from endangering throughout our lifetime

Synopsis 16 ❖ Returning to Tao

Being empty and still are being relatively free of concepts, desires and impulses. Rather than being experiences of emptiness and stillness, being empty and still are the emptiness and stillness of experiences. Emptiness and stillness are the plenum void and plenum stasis of perfectly balanced thoughts, feelings and actions that are enabling a receptive witnessing and a responsive following of the natural comings and goings of alternating and flowing experiencing. Living beings are being born, growing, aging and dying which is an endless cycling of originating from and returning to Tao, the primordial Origin, Root-Source and Eternal Constant. Embodying, according with and returning to Tao are a progression from vacuity and tranquility to originality, constancy, luminosity, totality, impartiality, universality, naturalness, harmony and longevity; free from endangering living throughout our lifetime.

Commentary 16 ❖ Returning to Tao

Wise attenders are:

Clearing their minds of concepts, emptying their hearts of desires and stilling their wills of impulses and are witnessing and following the lives of human beings and the constant, continual and continuous presencing, proceeding, unfolding, progressing, cycling and completing of the myriad ongoing experiential phenomena of the attending relationship/process just as they are.

Experiencing that the attending relationship/process is a seamless cycling from the mysterious originating of experiential phenomena, through their miraculous forming and marvelously manifesting to their magnificent completion and, as such, is transient, everchanging and transforming.

Welcoming and embracing all experiences in the attending relationship/process openly, calmly, originally, constantly, radiantly, inclusively, impartially, universally, naturally, harmoniously, completely and safely.

EXPERIENCE 17

DEVELOPED GOVERNING

Most developed governing
Is barely being known by people
Next is being loved and praised
Next is being feared
Least developed governing
Is being despised

When we are not trusting others
Then others are not trusting us

We are minimizing words
We are completing works
And people are saying
Everything is happening naturally
Or being done by themselves

SYNOPSIS 17 ❖ DEVELOPED GOVERNING

Depending upon the degree and extent of the development of leaders; their governing, ordering and regulating are ranging from being Tao-like, i.e., relatively anonymous, to benevolence that is loved and praised, to righteousness that is feared, to propriety that is despised. The most developed governing is being non-hierarchical, non-authoritarian, low-profile, minimally impactful, trusting and non-interfering. People are experiencing relatively leaderless governing and are feeling that either it is happening naturally or they are self-regulating.

COMMENTARY 17 ❖ DEVELOPED GOVERNING

Wise attenders are:

Maintaining a low-key and low-impact profile in the attending relationship/process by making few verbalizations and concise interventions and are relatively unobtrusive, non-confrontive, non-intrusive and non-invasive without needs to be recognized for doing good, validated for being right or complied with for being proper which, respectively, are only eliciting praise, fear and contempt in human beings.

Establishing good rapport, cooperative and collaborative interpersonal relationships and working therapeutic alliances based upon mutual and reciprocal trust and not exploiting power differentials or engaging in power struggles in the attending relationship/process.

Experiencing that creating safety, having interest, being non-directive, asking open-ended questions, making empathic reflections and giving encouragement and support are allowing human beings to naturally, openly and uniquely self-disclose, self-explore, self-discover and self-regulate; to own originating their experiences, activities and outcomes and to take greater responsibility for them.

EXPERIENCE 18

FORGETTING TAO

When we are forgetting Tao
Benevolence and righteousness are appearing

When we are professing doctrines
Great hypocricies and true believers are appearing

When we are dehumanizing families
Dutiful parents and obedient children are appearing

When we are corrupting countries
Loyal officials and patriotic citizens are appearing

Synopsis 18 ❖ Forgetting Tao

As Tao is progressively being forgotten, dogmatized, dehumanized and corrupted; there is a decline into benevolence and righteousness, a degeneration into hypocrisy, a deterioration into propriety and a disintegration into false loyalty. When Tao is not being present in our world, there is devolution and the world is being populated by do-gooders and be-righters, hypocrits and fanatics, obligees and conformists and loyalists and patriots. There is an unnaturalness and artificiality that is resulting in a progressive loss of human kindness and fairness, truth and wisdom, loving and respecting, fidelity and community and the Spirit, Heart and Soul of Tao.[23]

Commentary 18 ❖ Forgetting Tao

Wise attenders are:

Remembering and not eclipsing or displacing their identifying *as* Tao by only doing good, being right and being proper in the attending relationship/process and by professing dogmas, dehumanizing human beings and politicizing treatment.

Not instituting and perpetuating a devolved attending relationship/process involving rigid rules, fixed roles and prescribed rituals and only orthodox theories, standardized techniques, formal interactions and conventional interventions.

Not being interested in having a following and clientele of affectionate and devoted, indoctrinated and entranced, compliant and obedient, disempowered and dependent and partisan and sectarian human beings who are being so at the expense of their dignity, worth and unique reality, truth, authenticity, integrity, genius and beauty.

CHING

LITERARY CLASSIC/SCRIPTURE/CANON
PASS THROUGH/EXPERIENCE/UNDERGO
STANDARD/REGULATE/TRANSACT
LONGITUDE/WARP/MERIDIANS/VEINS
CONSTANT/RECURRING

DEEP/UNDERGROUND FLOWING WATERCOURSES
AND LONG/INTERWEAVING PASSAGEWAYS OF
EXPERIENCING.

EXPERIENCE 19

EMBODYING SIMPLICITY

Mobility is overcoming cold
Serenity is overcoming heat
Being clear and calm
Is being a model for our world
As people:
Abandoning sageliness and saintliness
We are benefiting one hundred fold
Relinquishing benevolence and righteousness
We are returning to natural lovingness
Eliminating craftiness and profiteering
We are discontinuing clever thievery

These three measures are insufficient externals

As people, let us be:
Discerning plainness
Embodying simplicity
Reducing selfishness
Diminishing desiring

Synopsis 19 ❖ Embodying Simplicity

As sageliness, saintliness, benevolence, righteousness, craftiness and profiteering are being given up, we are experiencing the great benefits of Sacredness, inner wisdom, natural loving, genuine relationships and honest working. We are further encouraged to be adopting and living an inner-oriented life of plainness, simplicity, reduced self-interest and diminished desiring.

Commentary 19 ❖ Embodying Simplicity

Wise attenders are:

Benefiting human beings in the attending relationship/process by not being sagely or saintly, by not espousing dogmatic theories and perpetrating ritualistic techniques, by not doing 'good' and being 'right' and by not devising clever agendas and executing crafty strategies designed to achieve desired outcomes, reinforce an ego-ideal or self-image or to realize monetary gain or professional fame.

Experiencing that, by not doing the above, human beings are being able to acknowledge, accept, allow and appreciate the simplicity, sufficiency, selflessness and lovingness of their innermost, deepest, centermost, truest and utmost Tao-nature or Virtuosity/Te.

Not being 'know it alls', 'do-gooders and 'rip offs' by conducting the attending relationship/process as if were a craft, trade or business skillfully packaged, adroitly marketed and profitably sold to achieve self-interests, professional fame and financial gain by exploiting and capitalizing on the limitations, woundings and sufferings of needful human beings.

EXPERIENCE 20

NOURISHING TAO

Relinquishing learnedness and propriety
There is no regretting
How different are yes and yeh?
How similar are good and bad?

What people are fearing
Must I be fearing?
How ridiculous!

Other people are being happy
Feasting at festive banquets
Climbing up flowery terraces
I alone am unmoving, showing no signs
Like an infant, not yet imitating
Downcast, like a homeless vagrant

Other people are having plenty
I alone am lacking everything
Mine is the heart-mind of a fool
Muddled and bewildered

Other people are being bright
I alone am being dark
Other people are being sharp
I alone am being dull

Drifting as the boundless sea
Aimless as the limitless wind
Other people are making plans
I alone am goalless

I alone am differing from other people
In drawing nourishment from Mother Tao

SYNOPSIS 20 ❖ NOURISHING TAO

We are being encouraged to question and/or relinquish the pretense of making intellectual distinctions between the formal and the colloquial and of making evaluative judgments about what is good and bad. The author is modeling detaching from and disidentifying with the beliefs, fears, conventions, activities, behaviors and characteristics of the masses of collective humanity and their festivities, amusements, opulence, brilliantness, astuteness and ambitions. By contrast, the author is modeling being an artless infant, homeless vagrant, witless dullard and aimless drifter; wandering and wondering in Nature's spacious wilderness, solely and uniquely nourished and fully and happily sustained by Mother Tao.

COMMENTARY 20 ❖ NOURISHING TAO

Wise attenders are:

Not making extraneous intellectualized distinctions and irrelevant value judgments about the behaviors and life styles of human beings and are not identifying with their fears or harboring counterphobic attitudes toward irrationality, abnormality, deviancy or insanity.

Not identifying with the typical amusements and entertainments, collective values and social conventions or personal demeanors and activities of the general public and, perhaps, some professional colleagues.

Not striving for brilliant, incisive and astute interpretations or implementing preplanned, goal-directed and strategic interventions; are allowing purposes and objectives to collaboratively and naturally arise from the attending relationship/process; are maintaining free-floating/evenly hovering attention and innocent wonder and are drawing sustaining nourishment and energetic support from Mother Tao.

EXPERIENCE 21

INNER LIGHT OF TAO

The intrinsic nature of Great Virtuosity
Is uniquely individualizing Tao alone

Tao is elusive, indistinct
Indistinct, elusive
Yet within it are images
Elusive, indistinct
Yet within it are beings
Deep and dark
Yet within it are energies
Vital and efficacious

From ancient times until right now
Its name is constantly reappearing
By which we are witnessing
The originating of all beings

How can all beginnings be experienced?
Through and as 'This'

SYNOPSIS 21 ❖ INNER LIGHT OF TAO

The intrinsically energetic nature and vitally efficacious power of Virtuosity/Te are the unique instantiating, individualizing[24] and personifying of profoundly mysterious and subtly elusive Tao. Tao, as vital Primordial Ch'i energy, is the original creative source and ultimate re-source of all beings and the inborn nature, unique reality and inner truth of their being. We are experiencing original and originating Tao; in, through and *as* the light of our innermost, deepest, centermost, truest and utmost Tao-Being or Virtuosity/Te just *as* it is; immediately, concretely and directly; in the present here-now moments of our living, i.e., all 'This' that is within, right here and right now.

COMMENTARY 21 ❖ INNER LIGHT OF TAO

Wise attenders are:

Being and living their Virtuosity/Te by uniquely individualizing, embodying, internalizing, assimilating, personifying and identifying *as* constant, original and originating Tao, the creative source of, and energetic re-source for, human beings.

Experiencing that, even though Tao is not an object-content or thing-event in ordinary human consciousness; its inner images, inherent being and intrinsic energies are constituting the Spirit, Heart and Soul of the human beings whose lives they are witnessing and participating in.

Perhaps, like Tao, seeming indistinct and elusive to human beings who, nonetheless, are not denying experiencing their radiant energy, the creative and efficacious power of their authentic presence and their pervasive in-fluence and versatile genius in the inner life of the attending relationship/process.

EXPERIENCE 22

EMBODYING ONE

Cycling, completing
Bending, straightening
Emptying, fulfilling
Exhausting, renewing

Having little, obtaining more
Having much, becoming confused

As wise human beings, we are:
Embodying One
And being world models
Not displaying and are shining
Not asserting and are attracting
Not boasting and are receiving
Not parading and are enduring
Not contending with anyone
And no one is contending with us

This ancient saying:
Cycling, being complete
No idle words
Being complete is re-turning

SYNOPSIS 22 ❖ EMBODYING ONE

Bipolar experiences are inseparable complements that are recip-rocal and naturally compensating. They reach a maximum, revert to their counterpart and return to their origin, e.g., in the Yin/Yang Ch'i alternations of night/day, waxing/waning of the moon, ebbing/flow-ing of tides, peaking/troughing of waves, the systolic/diastolic heart-beat, the inspiration/expiration of breath and the cycling of seasons. Cycling, bending, emptying and exhausting are reverting to complet-ing, straightening, fulfilling and renewing and vice versa. Wise human beings are being world models by embodying One, the transpolar unity and identity, that is unifying the myriad bipolarities within human experience and existence. They are not displaying, asserting, boasting, parading and contending and, hence, are shining, attracting, receiv-ing, enduring and at peace. Cycling is completing, which is an endless returning. What is beginning as a bipolarity is ending as circularity. In spherical circularity or cycling, e.g., rotating, revolving and orbiting, beginnings are endings and endings are completions but also are tran-sitions to new beginnings. Taking turns are completed in returning, the uni-verse is One-turning and our precious lives are our one-turn.

COMMENTARY 22 ❖ EMBODYING ONE

Wise attenders are:

Allowing the various bipolarities of the attending relationship/ process to naturally run their course, alternate to their complement, cycle and return and are straightening out, fulfilling, renewing and completing contents, interactions, processes and activities by letting them be naturally yielding, emptying, used up and cycling, e.g., ten-sions relax, fevers break, pain subsides, symptoms remit, wounds heal and illness is reverting to health in the healing crisis.

Modeling unconfusing simplifying by not displaying talents, asserting positions, boasting about accomplishments, parading suc-cesses or contending issues and, hence, are being radiantly luminous, magnetically attracting, openly receiving and durably connecting with human beings and harmoniously free of contending.

Constantly, continually and continuously facilitating good com-pletions and closures of wise attending experiences, are returning to origins and new beginnings and are experiencing that often when the attending relationship/process is nearing its ending there is a re-in-troduction of the presenting issues and symptoms of human beings.

EXPERIENCE **23**

CORRESPONDING IDENTITIES

Nature is not continually expressing itself
Windstorms are not lasting all morning
Rainstorms are not lasting all evening

What is causing this?
Heaven-Earth is causing this
If Heaven-Earth is not making events last long
How can we, as people, be doing so?

Following Tao is identifying with/as Tao
Following Virtuosity is identifying with/as Virtuosity
Following loss is identifying with/as loss

Tao is endowing whomever is becoming Tao
Virtuosity is empowering whomever is becoming Virtuosity
Loss is abandoning whomever is becoming loss

When we are not trusting others
Then others are not trusting us

Synopsis 23 ❖ Corresponding Identities

Most all natural phenomena are essentially and ultimately temporary and transient. We are not able to make the natural changings of phenomena last longer than their time limits. Our own human experiences and lives are having their own time and also are not lasting long. We are becoming and being whatever we are following and identifying with. When we are identifying with/*as* Tao, Virtuosity/Te or loss; we are becoming and being Tao, Virtuosity/Te or loss. When we are not trusting, we are not identifying with/*as* trust and will be distrusted or mistrusted.

Commentary 23 ❖ Corresponding Identities

Wise attenders are:

Not interfering with the natural transiency of the initiating, proceeding, unfolding, progressing, completing and terminating of the attending relationship/process by making extended monologues, lengthy interpretations and interactions, prolonged interventions, chronic prognoses and long-term recommendations.

Trusting that, as in the natural cyclical returning of phenomena, experiences are self-limiting and self-correcting, e.g., anxiety dissipates, depression lifts, pain subsides, symptoms remit, questions are answered, problems are solved, conflicts are resolved and wounds heal; and that the turn around time is shortened when the conditions and issues are openly accepted and fully experienced rather than ignored, denied, resisted, avoided or over-treated.

Identifying *as* the abundant sufficiency of Tao and the potent efficacy of Virtuosity/Te rather than exclusively as trauma, abuse, wounding, illness, failure, loss, deficiency, etc. and, as such, are being models for the human beings in their care who are trusting and being endowed (en-Tao-ed) and empowered, e.g., when identifying as illness, illness is only illness; when identifying *as* Virtuosity/Te, illness is a wake-up call and opportunity; when identifying *as* Tao, illness also is Tao.

EXPERIENCE 24

BEING SUFFICIENT

As people:
When reaching, we are not solid
When striding, we are not fluid

As people:
When displaying, we are not shining
When asserting, we are not attracting
When boasting, we are not receiving
When parading, we are not enduring

From the standpoint of Tao
These are excessive wasteful actions
To be avoiding

As wise human beings
Who are embodying Tao
We are avoiding them

SYNOPSIS 24 ❖ BEING SUFFICIENT

Overextending is an ungrounded and uncentered action creating instability and imbalance. When we are displaying, asserting, boasting and parading, we are moving off ground and center and are not shining, attracting, receiving and enduring. These externally-oriented actions are excessive, extraneous, useless and wasteful and are not being indulged in by wise human beings embodying, internalizing, assimilating, personifying, enacting and identifying *as* Tao.

COMMENTARY 24 ❖ BEING SUFFICIENT

Wise attenders are:

Maintaining solidity, stability, flexibility and fluidity by not effortfully overextending groundednes and centeredness by reaching and striving for certain desired effects, results and outcomes, e.g., insights, catharses, breakthroughs or cures, that are only creating 'trying' experiences.

Avoiding excessive, counterproductive, unproductive and wasteful behaviors and actions such as displaying talents, asserting positions, boasting about accomplishments, parading successes or contending issues and, rather, are modeling their attendant radiance, magnetism, receptivity, durability and harmony for human beings and leaving space for them to contact, experience, own and express their unique reality, truth, beauty, ability and genius.

Modestly employing, appropriately timing, economically communicating, efficiently conducting and effectively concluding interactions and interventions; guided by Tao and their Virtuosity/Te without wasting their valuable time or that of the human beings with whom they are sharing the attending relationship/process.

EXPERIENCE 25

GREAT FOLLOWING

Here is This
Undifferentiated and complete
Preceding the birthing of Heaven-Earth
Independent, still, empty and unchanging
All-pervading and inexhaustible
It is Mother of all beings
Knowing it is truly unnamable
I am calling it Tao

Being invited to identify it
I am calling it Great
Being great is going on and on
Everflowing is being far-reaching
Going beyond is returning to Root-Source

Tao is great
Heaven is great
Earth is great
Human Being is great
These are the four great identities
Of our universe
And Human Being is one of them

Human Being is following Earth
Earth is following Heaven
Heaven is following Tao
Tao is following its own spontaneous Nature

SYNOPSIS 25 ❖ GREAT FOLLOWING

Tao is self-originating and independent, undifferentiated and unchanging, all-pervading and all-inclusive, still and empty, complete and inexhaustible. Tao is the absolute No-thingness (Wu Chi) and pure potentiality (Primordial Ch'i) that is antedating Heaven-Earth and is Mother of all beings, the open matrix of all Mysterious originating, Miraculous forming, Marvelous manifesting and Magnificent completing. Tao is unnamable and great and Tao, Heaven-Earth and Human Beings are all great. Being great is being everflowing, far-reaching and cyclically returning to itself. Heaven-Earth and Human Beings are Tao-like and share the same identity *as* Tao. Human Beings are following Earth, Earth is following Heaven, Heaven is following Tao and Tao is following its own spontaneous Nature, being of-itself-so (Tzu Jan) and *as*-itself-so.

COMMENTARY 25 ❖ GREAT FOLLOWING

Wise attenders are:

Identifying *as* the still and empty, undifferentiated and constant, all-pervading and all-including and complete and inexhaustible nature of Tao and its qualities of greatness, everflowingness, spaciousness and self-returning that are the origin, root-source and Mother of all human beings and all experiences in the attending relationship/process.

Identifying *as* the vastness, limitlessness, ongoingness and endlessness of Great Tao and are humbly participating as one of the universal greatnesses of Tao and Heaven-Earth and naturally sharing in the spontaneous operating, organizing, regulating and harmonizing of all within the universe.

Following the naturalness and spontaneity of their innermost, deepest, centermost, truest and utmost Tao-nature or Virtuosity/Te and are naturally allowing the attending relationship/process to be more spontaneously and vitally alive, creatively and inventively improvisational and novel and fresh rather than premeditated, preplanned, predetermined and predictable.

EXPERIENCE 26

GROUNDING AND CENTERING

Being heavy is the ground of lightness
Being still is the center of hastiness

As wise human beings, we are traveling all day
Without leaving a center of gravity

Though compelling sights are along the way
We are remaining undistracted and undisturbed
Like the lords of ten thousand chariots
Who cannot afford to be frivolous

Being too light is uprooting supporting ground
Being too hasty is unseating regulating center

SYNOPSIS 26 ❖ GROUNDING AND CENTERING

Wise human beings are being grounded and centered in their identifying *as* Tao as a solid foundational support and calm core connection. On wayfaring journeys, they are undistracted and undisturbed by compelling draws, pulls and side-shows of the external world. Wise human beings are remaining grounded and centered amid the multiplicity of worldly goings on and, like the lords of ten thousand chariots, cannot afford to be frivolous. They are living in a grounded center and centered ground between lightness and heaviness and stillness and hastiness and are being serenely serious and seriously serene.

COMMENTARY 26 ❖ GROUNDING AND CENTERING

Wise attenders are:

Being solidly grounded and calmly centered *as* Tao and are not being distracted, diverted, detained or disturbed by the many compelling phenomena, experiences and vicissitudes of the attending relationship/process, e.g., fascinating, unusual, exotic, strange and bizarre images, fantasies, associations, histories, memories, dreams and other object-contents.

Not being too light or hasty in reflections, interpretations, feedback, interactions, activities and interventions and risking becoming ungrounded and uncentered, e.g., through humorous interjections or half-baked formulations.

Respecting and honoring the experiences of human beings and not taking them lightly or frivolously or dismissing them quickly or hastily and risking disrupting the Tao-grounded support and Tao-centered regulating of the attending relationship/process and displacing the Tao-Selves of human beings.

EXPERIENCE 27

TEACHING AND LEARNING

As most developed travelers
We are leaving no tracks
As most developed speakers
We are creating no doubts
As most developed counters
We are needing no tallies

As most developed closers
We are using no locks
Yet doors cannot be opened
As most developed binders
We are using no knots
Yet books cannot be untied

As wise human beings:
We are continually assisting all people
None are being excluded
As wise human beings:
We are continually assisting all beings
None are being excluded
This is following Inner Light

As developed human beings:
We are teaching sources for undeveloped ones
As undeveloped human beings
We are learning resources for developed ones
Not valuing such teaching sources
Not valuing such learning resources
We are foolishly deviating
Despite being educated

This is the essential Secret

Synopsis 27 ❖ Teaching and Learning

Most developed human beings are being complete in the here and now and are not requiring external material objects or creating extraneous visible residues. Living life is a deeply internal and invisible process that nonetheless is having profound external and visible effects. Wise human beings are following the Inner Light of Tao and are continually assisting human beings and other beings without judgment, discrimination, preference, favoritism or exception. To not be valuing human beings as teaching sources and learning resources is to be unwisely deviating from developing oneself and other human beings in spite of knowing better.

Commentary 27 ❖ Teaching and Learning

Wise attenders are:

Being clear, contactful and connected with good closures and completions in their reflections and interactions with human beings without restricting and limiting or foreclosing and aborting their experiencing by making conclusive interpretations and using contrived interventions to lock in understandings or tie up loose ends.

Following the Inner Light of Tao and not excluding any human being from engaging in and benefiting from being assisted in the attending relationship/process and are not pathologizing, infantalizing, patronizing, marginalizing, stigmatizing, criminalizing, demonizing, victimizing or otherwise dehumanizing any human being.

Understanding, valuing and experiencing the attending relationship/process as a synchronistic meeting of human beings who are engaging in a mutual, equal and reciprocal intersubjective teaching and learning experience for the benefit of each and every one in ways that are going far beyond traditional role distinctions and transference/countertransference relationships.

CH'I

Breath
Air/steam/gas/vapor/ether
Vital energy/life force
Cosmic Spirit

Life-constituting/pervading/sustaining
Animating/vitalizing/nourishing
Cosmic order/natural laws/world process
Ubiquitous/ever-present/ever-circulating
Primordial/non-material/undifferentiated
Acquired/material/differentiated
Manner/temper
2 Principles (Yin and Yang)
Yin/Yang Ch'i/Wu Wei Ch'i
Synonymous with transcendent/immanent Tao

Yin/Yang Ch'i Dynamics	*Wu Wei Ch'i Kinetics*
Generating/originating	**Suitable/appropriate**
Forming/transforming	**Necessary/essential**
Alternating/reciprocating	**Flowing/circulating**
Compensating/equalizing	**Seamless/continuous**
Balancing/centering	**Frictionless/effortless**
Voiding/reversing	**Cycling/returning**
Tao-regulated interactions	**Tao-sourced activities**

EXPERIENCE 28

KNOWING AND EMBODYING

Knowing masculine
Embodying feminine
Being valleys receiving our world
Being valleys of our world
We are not straying from eternal Virtuosity
And are returning to this Original State

Knowing light
Embodying dark
Beings models guiding our world
Being models of our world
We are not deviating from constant Virtuosity
And are returning to this Ultimate State

Knowing splendor
Embodying humility
Being streams nourishing our world
Being streams of our world
We are not departing from abundant Virtuosity
And are returning to this Natural State

As primordial simplicity is differentiating
It is becoming discrete and concrete objects
Which, as wise human beings, we are utilizing
As chief instruments for developing people

Most developed governing
Is not cutting up

SYNOPSIS 28 ❖ KNOWING AND EMBODYING

Outwardly knowing masculine, light and splendor and inwardly embodying feminine, dark and humility are not leaving eternal, constant and abundant Virtuosity/Te and are returning to the originality, ultimacy and naturalness of Tao. When the Primordial Simplicity of Nondual Tao is differentiated into separate objects, wise human beings are using these rich and varied phenomena for developing human beings and restoring wholeness and integrity. Wise human beings are receiving, nourishing and guiding human beings and assisting their returning to Original, Ultimate and Natural Tao.

COMMENTARY 28 ❖ KNOWING AND EMBODYING

Wise attenders are:

Embodying the inner Yin dimension of Tao, i.e., its feminine, dark and humble quality and are knowing the outer Yang dimension of Tao, i.e., its masculine, light and splendrous quality and are integrating the Yin/Yang bipolarities of body-mind, unconscious-conscious and Soul-Spirit.

Experiencing their Virtuosity/Te as being like eternally deep valleys, constantly present models and abundantly flowing streams receiving, guiding and nourishing human beings and assisting them in not straying, deviating and departing from their own Virtuosity/Te and in returning to the originality, ultimacy and naturalness of the Tao-State of Being.

Not considering any and all of the many experiential phenomena and object-contents occurring in the attending relationship/process necessarily as ends in themselves but, rather, as opportunities, instruments and vehicles to be used for assisting human beings in the awareness, developing and restoring of their unity, integrity and wholeness, i.e., their Nondual Reality and Integral Harmony.

EXPERIENCE 29

SACRED VESSEL

Desiring to take over our world
Trying to control and manipulate it
I am seeing that we cannot be succeeding
Our world is a Sacred vessel
Not for us to be interfering with
Acting upon it is ruining it
Holding onto it is losing it

Among all beings in our world
Some are leading, others are following
Some are struggling, others are relaxing
Some are growing, others are declining
Some are succeeding, others are failing

As wise human beings, we are avoiding
Extremes, excesses, extravagances

Synopsis 29 ❖ Sacred Vessel

Our world is a Sacred vessel not to be possessed, controlled or manipulated. Interfering with our world, i.e., meddling, tampering, tinkering and toying with it, is harming, ruining and losing it. Just *as* it is, our world is naturally populated by human beings who are embodying various bipolar characteristics such as leading-following, struggling-relaxing, growing-declining and succeeding-failing. Wise human beings are living moderately balanced and centered amid these and other bipolarities and are avoiding extremes, excesses and extravagances.

Commentary 29 ❖ Sacred Vessel

Wise attenders are:

Accepting the Sacred vessel of the attending relationshp/process just *as* it is and are not holding onto or acting upon it by trying to control, force, change, manipulate and direct it by making interfering interventions.

Allowing the attending relationship/process to naturally dynamically alternate between being structured and unstructured, difficult and easy, progressing and regressing, succeeding and failing, etc..

Avoiding making extreme interpretations, excessive interactions and extravagant interventions designed to motivate, confront and challenge human beings and, rather, are being receptive and responsive to just the ways in which the attending relationship/process is naturally unfolding and proceeding so that its reality, actuality and truth are not ruined or lost.

NON-FORCING, NON-OVERDOING

Using Tao in assisting leaders
Is not governing our world by forcing
Using force is recoiling on its users

Where forces are dwelling
Brambles are growing
Where forces are fighting
Famines are following

When some force must be used
To achieve necessary results
It is used only reluctantly and stopped
Without priding, boasting, parading
Or dominating human beings

Overdeveloping power is accelerating decay
This is not according with Tao
What is not following Tao
Is quickly coming to an early ending[25]

Synopsis 30 ❖ Non-Forcing, Non-Overdoing

Regulating by Tao is allowing balance and harmony to come about naturally without controlling by forcing or fighting. Using force for fighting is involving thorny entanglements and is resulting in devasting impoverishment of human beings. Regretably, necessary results may need to be achieved through the use of force but without continuing it, priding, boasting, parading or dominating. Overdeveloping power and using force are accelerating a decline in the natural self-regulating processes of Tao and are resulting in rapid and premature demise and not reaching Tao.

Commentary 30 ❖ Non-Forcing, Non-Overdoing

Wise attenders are:

Identifying *as* Tao and Virtuosity/Te and are not controlling human beings or the attending relationship/process by forcing anything to occur, which is only creating defensive resistance, negative transference reactions, power struggles and rebellious acting-out that are entangling and impoverishing human beings.

Not using any accorded status, exploiting any power differentials or misusing their power to forcefully dominate or manipulate the attending relationship/process in order to achieve certain desired effects, results and outcomes or to pride in certain ego-ideals, self-images and professional personas.

Not forcefully using the potency and efficacy of their Virtuosity/ Te to produce changes in human beings or the attending relationship/ process and are experiencing that overdeveloping and overusing their regulating power are violating the natural unfolding of both and are resulting in empathic failure, derailed process, accelerated decline and early termination.

EXPERIENCE 31

VICTORIES ARE FUNERALS

Weapons are instruments of disaster
As most developed human beings,
We are deploring them and their use
Embodying Tao, we are living without them

As leaders, we are:
Honoring the left at home
Honoring the right at war

Weapons are instruments of disaster
As most developed leaders,
Should we be required to use them,
It is as a last resort
And with utmost restraint

Even if victorious,
As most developed leaders,
We are not enjoying it
Enjoying victory is enjoying slaughtering
Enjoying slaughtering,
We are not succeeding in the world

We are honoring:
The left at fortunate events
The right at unfortunate events
Under generals are standing on the left
Chief generals are standing on the right
An arrangement like that of a funeral

Slaughtering multitudes of human beings
Is bringing grief and sorrow
We are treating victories as funerals

Synopsis 31 ❖ Victories are Funerals

Using weapons in fighting and warring against enemies is a disaster involving slaughtering human beings. Wise human beings are not using weapons as a means to the end of achieving and celebrating victories in battles that are defeating and conquering enemies. They are engaging in wayfaring and not warfaring. The left side is symbolizing peace at home, good fortune and living and the right side is symbolizing war in the field, bad fortune and killing. Both victories and funerals are being honored on the right side, the side of dying, sorrowing and grieving.

Commentary 31 ❖ Victories are Funerals

Wise attenders are:

Identifying *as* Tao, are not taking warfare as a paradigm for the attending relationship/process, and are not having an arsenal of powerful weapons or a manual of tactical maneuvers to wage military missions, operations and campaigns against, or assaults upon, psychological 'enemies,' e.g., to fight impulses, battle problems, combat addictions, disarm defenses, attack armoring, subdue resistance, overthrow symptoms, beat illness, defeat patterns, overcome conflicts, conquer depression, quell anxiety, kill pain, etc..

Only using powerful tools, methods and processes with restraint to stabilize human beings in necessary crisis management and emergency situations without violating their dignity, integrity, autonomy and humanity.

Acknowledging, honoring and grieving the collatoral damage and body count of wounded and dead egos accompanying the process of human beings winning back and liberating their real, true, genuine and authentic Selves.

EXPERIENCE 32

SWEET DEW, FLOWING HOME

Tao is constant and unnamable
Although simple and subtle,
No one in our world is mastering it
As leaders, when we are embodying it,
All beings are according spontaneously

Heaven-Earth is harmonizing
Gently raining down sweet dew
Which, without commanding,
Is falling impartially and equally
Upon all beings

Once wholeness is differentiated,
Defining names are endlessly given
Is it not time to stop?
Knowing when to stop
Is freeing us from endangering

All beings in our world
Are coming home to Tao
Like mountain valley streams
Are flowing into the sea

SYNOPSIS 32 ❖ SWEET DEW, FLOWING HOME

Tao is not being well known nor cultivated by human beings in our world. When embodied by leaders, all beings naturally and spontaneously are according with it, e.g., like a magnetic force field is energetically attracting, cohering and organizing iron filings. The harmonizing of Tao, as Heaven-Earth, is gently raining down sweet dew that is naturally falling impartially and equally upon all beings, even as we are differentiating its original wholeness into parts, naming and defining the parts, endangering our integrity and finding our way back home to Tao.

COMMENTARY 32 ❖ SWEET DEW, FLOWING HOME

Wise attenders are:

Being among a minority of colleagues who are aware of Tao; are identifying *as* Tao, are embodying the potency and efficacy of its presence and Virtuosity/Te and are experiencing that human beings are naturally and spontaneously aligning with, attuning to and according with its energetic magnetic field in-fluence (in-flowing) in the attending relationship/process.

Uniting and integrating their Heavenly-Earthly Tao-nature and are experiencing that the energies of Tao/Ch'i are naturally raining down upon human beings in the attending relationship/process with impartiality and equality and that it is not unusual for their questions, problems, issues, conflicts and symptoms to simply fall away due to their being incompatible with, and/or displaced by, the Ultimate Reality and vital Ch'i energies of Tao.

Experiencing that when the experiential phenomena of the attending relationship/process are being exclusively abstracted, objectified, differentiated, labeled and defined, e.g., as diagnostic categories, symptom complexes, clinical syndromes, pathological conditions, etiological factors, theoretical concepts, intrapsychic dynamics, interpersonal patterns, coping styles, etc.; it is time to stop such a proliferation that is endangering its wholeness as a context, crucible, medium and vehicle for human beings to naturally, effortlessly and seamlessly come home to their real, unique and true Tao-nature/Virtuosity/Te.

EXPERIENCE 33

SELF-CONTENTMENT

Understanding others
We are being intelligent
Understanding ourselves
We are being illuminated

Overcoming others
We are being outwardly powerful
Developing ourselves
We are being inwardly strong

Being content with ourselves
We are being wealthy

Using the force of will power
We may be achieving objectives
But connecting with Tao's place
We are enduring

Dying without dying
We are being immortal

SYNOPSIS 33 ❖ SELF-CONTENTMENT

Cultivating and developing ourselves are a process of self-under-standing and self-regulating that is illuminating and strengthening. Being content with who we are being is reflecting real wealth, true adequacy and genuine sufficiency. Forcing self-developing is just another fictitious ego-project that only is conceiving an illusion of attainment. No amount of intentional forcing can be making an ego create a Self, just as images, shadows, echoes and things are all derived effects that cannot, respectively create form, light, sound and Tao. Being inwardly connected with and identifying *as* Tao are allowing our ego to develop naturally and completely. As the caterpillar is dying to the butterfly, through orderly metamorphic stages of larva, cocoon, pupa/chrysalis and imago, so is the ego progressively transforming and dying to timeless and endless Tao, if we let it.

COMMENTARY 33 ❖ SELF-CONTENTMENT

Wise attenders are:

Supporting, assisting and facilitating human beings in self-under-standing and self-developing in inwardly illuminating and strength-ening ways that entail the courageous determination, personal power and spiritual fortitude needed for overcoming psychosocial condition-ing and for cultivating psychospiritual developing.

Utilizing their deep unforced connection with Tao as the endur-ing ground, center and horizon of, and the constant source of and re-source for, attaining and experiencing lasting self-transformations rather than only using will power, catalytic tools and forceful pro-cesses to be achieving transient ego-projects and objectives.

Being sufficient and content with the richness and wealth of who they are just *as* they are; are not oppressing themselves and human beings with ideas of who they should, ought, might, may, could, will or must be; are not ignoring the Virtuosity/Te of their unique gifts, talents and genius; and are dying to their innermost, deepest, center-most, truest and utmost eternal and immortal Tao-nature.

GREAT FLOWING TAO

Great Tao is flowing everywhere
Far to the left, far to the right
It is giving life to all beings
And is not abandoning any

It is:
Completing its work
Without claiming credit
Nourishing all beings
Without possessing any

Asking nothing, without desiring
It is being called small
Receiving everything, without dominating
It is being called great

As wise human beings
We are not striving for greatness
And are being great

Synopsis 34 ❖ Great Flowing Tao

Tao is the universal, ubiquitous, all-pervading, flowing and circulating of Wu Wei Ch'i energy and the operating of Heaven-Earth that are constantly, continually and continuously originating, vitalizing, nourishing, sustaining, developing and completing the living reality and process of all beings. Tao is going about its work naturally, spontaneously and automatically; desiring and possessing nothing; receiving and returning everything without dominating, claiming, owning or crediting. As such, Tao is both empty and full, small and great. Wise human beings are being Tao-like and identifying *as* its minuteness and emptiness and its greatness and fullness without striving to do or be so.

Commentary 34 ❖ Great Flowing Tao

Wise attenders are:

Identifying *as* the all-pervading, everflowing, life-giving and life-sustaining energies of Tao that are never leaving human beings and are the real Origin and true Source of the attending relationship/process even when it may be embarassing, shameful, ugly, painful and regrettable.

Supporting, assisting and facilitating human beings without being attached or possessive and are conducting and completing the work of the attending relationship/process without claiming credit for its successful results.

Free of personal and/or professional desires for recognition, praise or fame and are receiving all human beings without subordinating and dominating any and, as such, are naturally being both insignificant and magnificent without striving to do or be either.

EXPERIENCE 35

MAGNETISM OF TAO

Around human beings
Embodying the great image of Tao
Our whole world is gathering

Gathering and not being endangered
Being secure, satisfied and serene

Music and delicacies
Are attracting passing travelers
But what Tao is giving forth
Is minimal and flavorless

Looking for it, it is invisible
Listening for it, it is inaudible
Yet utilizing it, it is inexhaustible

SYNOPSIS 35 ❖ MAGNETISM OF TAO

Embodying Tao is like being a magnet naturally attracting and gathering human beings and bringing our separated, divided, fragmented and scattered selves back home to a connected center of safety, security, satisfaction, sufficiency and serenity. While entertainment and indulgences are distracting, diverting and detaining us along the ways of our journeying; it is the invisible, inaudible, intangible and insipid energy force-field of Tao that can be infallibly and inexhaustibly relied upon to be drawing, leading, guiding and returning us home to the deep inner core and central Heart of our essential Tao-nature and Tao-being.

COMMENTARY 35 ❖ MAGNETISM OF TAO

Wise attenders are:

Naturally and magnetically creating an in-fluencing (inflowing) and con-fluencing (flowing together) that are attracting human beings to them by their embodying, personifying, enacting and identifying *as* Tao and the Virtuosity/Te of their innermost, deepest, centermost, truest and utmost Tao-nature.

Experiencing that human beings are feeling safe, secure, satisfied, sufficient and serene in their presence and are finding them to be valuable, useful and effective resources for their developing, even though they are appearing to be quite ordinary human beings without any particular outstanding visible characteristics or tangible abilities.

Not being distracted, diverted, deviated and detained by seductive and exciting phenomena and 'material' in the attending relationship/process and are remaining identified *as* invisible, inaudible, intangible and insipid Tao; its infallible and inexhaustible usefulness and the awesome Yin power of its feminine, magnetic, receptive and centripetal energy.

EXPERIENCE 36

SUBTLE ILLUMINATION

Shrinking is following expanding
Weakening is following strengthening
Abandoning is following promoting
Depriving is following indulging
This is subtle illuminating

Tender and yielding
Are overcoming
Hard and rigid

Fish are not leaving deep waters
We are not publically displaying
Powerful instruments of this State

SYNOPSIS 36 ❖ SUBTLE ILLUMINATION

The bipolar dynamics of Yin Ch'i/Yang Ch'i energies are complementary, reciprocal, alternating, compensatory and reversing. When one pole of a given bipolarity is reaching its maximum, it is naturally reverting to its corresponding complementary pole, e.g., when inhalation is turning into exhalation. Intentionally interfering with or manipulating the natural dynamic rhythm of alternations in order to accelerate polarity reversals are disrupting the process, e.g., when something is purposefully being expanded, strengthened, promoted or indulged; it is closer to being shrunk, weakened, abandoned or deprived. This is the subtle illuminating about not interfering with natural transformations occurring in their own ways, in their own times and at their own rates. Tenderness and yielding are naturally overcoming hardness and rigidity without introducing external catalysts to force or accelerate the process. The deeper inner-centered transformative Tao-power of Yin Ch'i/Yang Ch'i energies is not being publically displayed.

COMMENTARY 36 ❖ SUBTLE ILLUMINATION

Wise attenders are:

Accepting the compensating transforming of Yin Ch'i/Yang Ch'i energies and allowing the natural reversing of bipolar complements within human experience without trying to interfere with, manipulate or accelerate natural processes by forcing changes, e.g., ego-deflation, weakening, reduction and surrender are naturally following the extremes of ego-inflation, strengthening, enhancement and indulgence.

Experiencing that answers, solutions, resolutions and remissions are residing deep within the center of questions, problems, conflicts and symptoms (as depicted in the Supreme Ultimate/ T'ai Chi symbol) and are naturally reaching their extreme and reverting to their complements, e.g., in the healing crisis where when illness is fully experienced, it naturally is reverting to healthiness, as difficult as it is to be allowing the condition to run its course without medicinal intervention.

Experiencing that the deeper and watery Yin way of inwardness, softness, tenderness, gentleness and yielding is naturally overcoming the higher and fiery Yang way of outwardness, hardness, toughness, roughness and rigidity and are not leaving their inner depths and pubically displaying the potency and efficacy of their Virtuosity/Te, lest it become a technique.

YIN	YANG
陰	陽

YIN	**YANG**
Shady/dark/cloudy/cold	Sunny/bright/clear/hot
Hidden/behind/below	Overt/front/above
Female principle in Nature	Male principle in Nature[26]
Other worldly/death	This worldly/life
Earth/soil/Mother	Heaven/sky/Father
Matter/body/belly	Spirit/mind/head
Lunar/night/winter	Solar/day/summer
Inner/depth/center	Outer/surface/periphery
Soft/watery/wet	Firm/fiery/dry
Still/receptive/yielding	Moving/creative/asserting
Magnetic/centripetal	Dynamic/centrifugal
Contracting/condensing	Expanding/radiating
Ebbing/waning/troughing	Flowing/waxing/cresting
Valleys/canyons/caverns	Mountains/hills/mounds

EXPERIENCE 37

PRIMORDIAL SIMPLICITY

Tao is constantly not-doing any-'thing'
Yet no-thing is being left undone
As leaders, when we are embodying it
All beings are transforming spontaneously

After developing naturally,
If desires are again stirring
We are quieting them
With Primordial Simplicity

Primordial Simplicity is being desireless
Being desireless is being at peace
Our world is settling of its own accord

Synopsis 37 ❖ Primordial Simplicity

The constant ongoing activity of Tao is naturally, effortlessly, continually and seamlessly originating, regulating, developing, transforming and completing all beings. When leaders are embodying Tao and its Yin/Yang Ch'i dynamics and Wu Wei Ch'i kinetics, all beings are spontaneously transforming into their unique being and true nature. Fluctuations in the developmental process of authentic being and living are naturally self-corrected by returning to experiencing the primordial simplicity of Tao which is desireless, sufficient and at peace without needing to know, have, do or be any 'thing' in particular. In this way, all beings and our world are settling of themselves so and of their own accord with appropriate coordination, communication, collaboration and cooperation.

Commentary 37 ❖ Primordial Simplicity

Wise attenders are:

Identifying *as* Tao and its dynamic-kinetic activities and operations and are not making purposeful and planned or taking devised and contrived actions by using interventions that are interfering with the natural proceeding, unfolding, developing and progressing of the attending relationship/process.

Experiencing that; when they are embodying Tao and clearing concepts, emptying desires, stilling impulses and uniting separations; human beings are naturally and spontaneously transforming and developing on their own, of themselves so and of their own accord/ Tzu Jan.

Experiencing that, when identified *as* the desirelesss sufficiency and peaceful tranquility of the Primordial Simplicity and wholeness of Tao, they are being able to be a balancing, centering, harmonizing and calming influence upon human beings.

EXPERIENCE **38**

LOSING VIRTUOSITY

Most developed Virtuosity is not displaying it
And so is being the highest Virtuosity
Least developed Virtuosity is displaying it
And so is being the lowest Virtuosity

As human beings of highest Virtuosity
We are not acting nor having needs to be doing
As people of lowest Virtuosity
We are acting and having needs to be doing

As people of most developed benevolence
We are acting but not having needs to be doing
As people of most developed righteousness
We are acting and having needs to be doing
As people of most developed propriety
We are acting and even forcing responses

When we are losing Tao, Virtuosity is appearing
When we are losing Virtuosity, benevolence is appearing
When we are losing benevolence, righteousness is appearing
When we are losing righteousness, propriety is appearing
Now, propriety is only the superficial veneer
Of real loyalty and true fidelity
And the beginning of disaster

Foreknowledge is only an ornamental flowering of Tao
And the beginning of ignorance

As most developed human beings, we are:
Dwelling in kernal not husk
Dwelling in fruit not flower
Rejecting the outer 'that'
Accepting the inner 'This'

SYNOPSIS 38 ❖ LOSING VIRTUOSITY

Most developed Virtuosity/Te is not displaying it and not acting or needing to be doing. Lesser developed Virtuosity/Te is displaying it and acting and needing to be doing what is good, right and proper. When Tao is being lost, benevolence, righteousness and propriety are progressively appearing and are ending in the disaster of false loyalty and infidelity. Wise human beings are dwelling in the substantial inner Heart of Original Tao and not in its superficial outer coverings, i.e., its kernal and fruit and not its husks and flowerings; its true wisdom and not its foreknowledge. They are rejecting externalized objectifications of Tao and Virtuosity/Te and are accepting internalized identifications *as* Tao and Virtuosity/Te.

COMMENTARY 38 ❖ LOSING VIRTUOSITY

Wise attenders are:

Not displaying Virtuosity/Te; not acting purposefully; not having needs, motives and impulses to be doing any 'thing' in particular in the attending relationship/process and are simply allowing their open awareness and deep connection with human beings to naturally flow into appropriate, essential or necessary activity.

Free of desiring or needing to be good, right and proper with human beings in the sense of rigidly conforming to conventional notions of what is helpful, correct and acceptable in the conducting of the attending relationship/process but are, however, committed to ethical and moral standards, personal and professional integrity and behaving responsibly and accountably.

Not interested in instituting rigid rules, formal roles and fixed rituals that are only generating fear, dependency and compliance or resulting in resistance, rebelliousness and acting-out but are, however, interested in experiencing, sharing and living in the here and now *as* the substantial reality and truth of the Inner Heart of Tao.

EXPERIENCE 39

BEING ONENESS

Since ancient times
These are being One
Being Oneness:
Heaven is being clear
Earth is being stable
Spirits are being Sacred
Valleys are being fertile
Beings are being viable
Leaders are being virtuous
All are being so
Through being One

Not being clear, Heaven is cracking
Not being stable, Earth is quaking
Not being Sacred, spirits are desisting
Not being fertile, valleys are drying up
Not being viable, beings are dying out
Not being virtuous, leaders are falling

Great is having its foundation in humble
High is having its foundation in low
As leaders, we are calling ourselves
Orphaned, widowed and destitute
Is not this being rooted in humility?

The most praiseworthy human beings
Do not need or desire praise
We are not clinking like precious jade
We are not clunking like ordinary rock

Synopsis 39 ❖ Being Oneness

Being the Oneness of Tao is essentially and inwardly being our absolutely unique identity, individuality, integrity and potentiality, i.e., really being who we truly are, clearly, deeply, Sacredly, fully, vitally and virtuously. Wise and developed leaders, while praiseworthy, are humbly regarding themselves as alone, lonely and lacking and are being grounded and centered in Tao beyond both ordinary preciousness and precious ordinariness.

Commentary 39 ❖ Being Oneness

Wise attenders are:

Identifying *as* the Oneness of ancient Tao and the unity and identity of Heaven, Earth, Spirit, Nature, Beings and Human Beings.

Being One and their:

> Minds are clear, illuminating and not cracking
> Bodies are stable, supporting and not quaking
> Spirits are Sacred, energizing and not desisting
> Souls are fertile, nourishing and not drying up
> Beings are viable, vitalizing and not dying out
> Selves are virtuous, elevating and not falling

Experiencing that any greatness of their development is founded in humility, are considering themselves lacking and are being grounded and centered in/*as* One Tao beyond either the unrefined nature of their natural being or the refined culture of their precious Being.

EXPERIENCE 40

REVERSING AND RETURNING

Reversing and returning
Are the moving of Tao
Softening and yielding
Are the operating of Tao

All beings are birthing from Being
Being is birthing from Non-Being

SYNOPSIS 40 ❖ REVERSING AND RETURNING

Reciprocal reversing and softening and cyclical returning and yielding are the bipolar and alternating Yin/Yang Ch'i dynamics and the flowing and circulating Wu Wei Ch'i kinetics of the moving and operating of Tao in beings and the world, cosmos and multiverse. All beings are originating from the allness and differentiating fullness of the Being of Tao and the Being of Tao is originating from the No-Thingness and undifferentiated emptiness of the Non-Being of Tao, the Non-Ultimate/Wu Chi empty void of no form and the Supreme Ultimate/T'ai Chi plenum void of perfectly balanced form.

COMMENTARY 40 ❖ REVERSING AND RETURNING

Wise attenders are:

Doing no-'thing' that is interfering with the natural ego-defense softening of Yin/Yang Ch'i dynamics and the natural ego-resistance yielding of Wu Wei Ch'i flowing kinetics that are originating, forming, manifesting and completing all of the experiential phenomena of the attending relationship/process.

Allowing the experiential phenomena of the attending relationship/process to continually counterbalance, centralize, void and reverse to their complement and to continuously flow, circulate, cycle and return to their origin.

Experiencing that the experiential phenomena of the attending relationship/process are originating from the Supreme Ultimate Being of Tao/T'ai Chi which, in turn, is originating from the Non-Ultimate/Non-Being of Tao/Wu Chi.

EXPERIENCE 41

LAUGHING AT TAO

As developed human beings hearing of Tao
We are practicing it wholeheartedly
As average human beings hearing of Tao
We are remembering and forgetting it
As undeveloped people hearing of Tao
We are laughing loudly about it
If we are not laughing about it
It would not be Tao

Here is an ancient saying:
Bright Tao is appearing dim
Advanced Tao is appearing behind
Level Tao is appearing uneven
High Virtuosity is appearing lowly
Pure Virtuosity is appearing murky
Vast Virtuosity is appearing empty
Solid Virtuosity is appearing flimsy
True substance is appearing shaky

Great space is having no edges
Great talent is developing late
Great music is sounding faint
Great image is having no form

Tao is being hidden and unnamable
Yet Tao alone
Is developing and completing

SYNOPSIS 41 ❖ LAUGHING AT TAO

Our relationship with Tao is reflecting the relative degree of our development, ranging from wholehearted cultivating, through half-hearted practicing to outright ridiculing. The realities of Tao and Virtuosity/Te are paradoxical, often appearing outwardly as their less collectively valued bipolar complements, e.g., bright, advanced and level Tao can be appearing dim, behind and uneven and high, pure, vast, solid and true Virtuosity/Te can be appearing lowly, murky, empty, flimsy and shaky. Tao is transphenomenal and ineffable and its characteristics are boundlessness, limitlessness, timelessness, end-lessness and formlessness, yet it alone is originating, nourishing, sus-taining, supporting, developing, regulating and completing all beings, even those who are laughing at it.

COMMENTARY 41 ❖ LAUGHING AT TAO

Wise attenders are:

Wholeheartedly cultivating, diligently practicing and consciously identifying *as* Tao and are observing that many of their professional colleagues are being amused by the absurdity of integrating Tao and psychotherapy/counseling.

Experiencing that the qualities of Tao and Virtuosity/Te are often appearing in paradoxical forms that human beings may not be recog-nizing as indicative of positive charactristics of an effective attending relationship/process, e.g.,

Awarenesses may be appearing dim
Progress may be appearing slow
Process may be appearing bumpy
Feedback may be appearing obvious
Reflections may be appearing unclear
Insights may be appearing irrelevant
Stability may be appearing tenuous
Validity may be appearing tentative
Great therapy may be limitless
Real changes may be following
True growth may be subtle
Deep transformation may be invisible

Experiencing that the valences, vectors and trajectories and the contours, rhythms and harmonics of the attending relationship/process are spacious, fluid, open-ended, subtle and unnamable and that identifiable progress and transformation may take some time to appear and realize, much like the developing process of photo nega-tives in the darkroom.

EXPERIENCE 42

PROGRESSING OF TAO

Tao is birthing One
One is birthing Two
Two is birthing Three
Three is birthing all beings

All beings are:
Bearing dark Yin on their backs
Harboring bright Yang in their arms
Harmonizing these vital energies
Is bringing all beings to completion

As people, we are shunning
Being orphaned, widowed and destitute
Yet, as leaders, we are titling ourselves so

We are often gaining by losing
We are often losing by gaining

As ancient ones are teaching
So am I teaching once again
As aggressive violent people
We are coming to violent endings
This is my essential teaching

SYNOPSIS 42 ❖ PROGRESSING OF TAO

The cosmogonic sequencing of Tao is progressing from zero; the Non-Entity, Non-Ultimate and Great Void/Wu Chi to one; the unity, primordial energy and Great Monad/Yuan Ch'i; to two; the bipolarity, primal polarity and Great Dyad/Yin/Yang Ch'i to three; the trinity, Supreme Ultimate and Great Triad/T'ai Chi (Wu Chi + Yin Ch'i and Yang Ch'i); to the totality, 10,000 things and Great Myriad/Wan Wu.[27] All beings are, more or less, bearing Yin Ch'i energies and enfolding Yang Ch'i energies and harmonizing them in/as their central Axis, Pivot and Heart of Tao. Developed and wise leaders are humbly regarding themselves as alone, lonely and lacking; are paradoxically, gaining by decreasing, reducing and simplifying and are experiencing that aggression and violence are begetting aggression and violence and their perpetrators are coming to violent endings, dying as they have lived.

COMMENTARY 42 ❖ PROGRESSING OF TAO

Wise attenders are:

Identifying with the cosmogonic sequencing of Tao as being experienced in the originating, generating, forming, harmonizing and manifesting of all of the experiential phenomena of the attending relationship/process.

Experiencing their attending relationship with human beings to be an embodiment and personification of bipolar Yin Ch'i/Yang Ch'i dynamics characterized by intersubjective interacting, mutual exchanging, dialogical communicating, reciprocal interchanging and harmonic centering.

Being humble about intimate relationships and successful outcomes in the course of the attending relationship/process; are simplifying interactions and interventions; are experiencing set-backs, regressions and relapses as opening the way to advancings, progressings and recovery and are not making aggressive confrontations that are violating human beings.

EXPERIENCE 43

NON-BEING, NON-DOING

Softest beings in our world
Are overcoming hardest ones

Non-Being is entering
Where there is no-space

So, I am understanding
The usefulness of Non-Doing

Teaching without speaking
Practicing without acting
Rarely being realized
In our world

SYNOPSIS 43 ❖ NON-BEING, NON-DOING

The Non-Being, No-'thing'-ness, emptiness and softness of Tao are naturally overcoming the solidness, fullness and hardness of objects and beings in the world. The non-materiality and insubstantiality of Tao can enter where there are no openings, spaces or gaps without effort, resistance or friction. This is the usefulness of Non-Being and non-doing, the minimizing of intentional speaking and purposeful acting and the rare transmission of Tao through wordless teaching and formless practicing.

COMMENTARY 43 ❖ NON-BEING, NON-DOING

Wise attenders are:

Experiencing that soft ways, Yin ways and Wu Weis in the attending relationship/process are assisting human beings in softening and melting defenses and resistances, relaxing tensions and contractions and loosening blocks and stuckness, e.g., through warm contact, open inquiry, gentle interactions, empathic understanding, inviting possibilities, mild interventions, subtle evocations, encouraging support and silent appreciation.

Experiencing the efficacy of non-being and the utility of non-doing by creating spacious and empty openness and intentionless and purposeless stillness in the attending relationship/process that are allowing human beings to be gaining access to and entering into their inner worlds of experiencing; even when they are solidly defended; without effort, resistance or friction, e.g., through open contact, deep connection, clear awareness and full communication that are relevant, meaningful, effective, Consciousness-expanding, Self-transforming, Life-changing and priority-shifting and rarely realized to such a degree and so quickly in the ordinary world of psychotherapy/counseling.

EXPERIENCE 44

NON-HAVING

Self or fame, which is more near?
Life or wealth, which is more dear?
Gain or loss, which is more fear?

Desiring is costing a lot
Hoarding is losing a lot

Knowing what is enough
Is avoiding shaming
Knowing when to stop
Is avoiding endangering
And shortening one's life

Synopsis 44 ❖ Non-Having

Being oneself and living one's life are precious and sufficient enough rather than seeking, pursuing, acquiring, possessing and accumulating name, fame, gain and wealth. Such desiring and hoarding are ending up costing, wasting and losing a lot. Knowing self-sufficiency and self-limiting are avoiding shaming oneself and endangering and shortening one's life.

Commentary 44 ❖ Non-Having

Wise attenders are:

Not compromising themselves and their lives by attaching to attaining famous reputations or investing in achieving financial gains in the attending relationship/process, are not desiring to be or to have more than they are being and having and are experiencing the sufficiency of knowing when enough is enough re:,e.g., the number of referrals, quantity of successes, extent of recognition, amount of income, etc..

Modeling for human beings valuing themselves and their lives and the selves and lives of human beings and are not being professional personas in professional roles who, after working, are going home, changing clothes and then being their real selves and living their true lives.

Being self-limiting and self-sufficing with regard to the amount of interpretations, interactions and interventions in the attending relationship/process and are not setting up human beings for shame and failure that is endangering and rewounding them and bringing about their early termination.

EXPERIENCE 45

WORLD MODEL

Most complete is seeming incomplete
Yet its usefulness is infallible
Most sufficient is seeming insufficient
Yet its usefulness is inexhaustible

Great propriety is appearing bent
Great dexterity is appearing inept
Great oratory is appearing hesitant

Mobility is overcoming cold
Serenity is overcoming heat
Being clear and calm
Is being a model for our world

Synopsis 45 ❖ World Model

The completeness and sufficiency of Tao, paradoxically, may be appearing to be incomplete and insufficient, but their usefulness is infallible and inexhaustible. Also, paradoxically, great appropriateness, skillfulness and eloquence may be appearing to be awkward, clumsy and halting. The dynamic bipolar Yin Ch'i/Yang Ch'i energies of Tao are compensating and balancing, e.g., moving is overcoming cold and stilling is overcoming heat. By being clear and calm, developed human beings are being models for our world.

Commentary 45 ❖ World Model

Wise attenders are:

Experiencing that Tao and the Virtuosity/Te of their innermost, deepest, centermost, truest and utmost Tao-nature are the infallible and inexhaustible agency in the attending relationship/process, even though their potency and efficacy may be appearing to be incomplete and insufficent and may only be realized after it has terminated, like seeds are maturing sometime after planting and cultivating.

Experiencing that polished professional demeanors, adroit technical proficiencies, facile communication skills and cleverly crafted interventions are not true, genuine or honest and that, because of its according with and allowing of universal laws and organismic processes, the attending relationship/process may be appearing to be unrefined, unorthodox and uncertain in its spontaneity/Tzu Jan, improvisation and serendipity.

Allowing Yin Ch'i/Yang Ch'i interchanging dynamics to be naturally compensating and counterbalancing through their being both verbal and silent, active and inactive, interpreting and reflecting, initiating and responding, etc. and are being clear and calm models for human beings in the attending relationship/process.

WU

無

No-/not-
Non-/un-
Nothing
Non-being
None
Without

WEI

Be/become
Do/act
Act as/serve as
Make/cause
Protect/support/help
Practice/cultivate

Tao-enacting/Tao-sourced/natural activities
Nothing doing/no 'thing'-doing/no-'thing' doing
Without 'doing'/acting/making
Without/not- / non-
intending/planning/strategizing
devising/contriving/implementing/executing
fabricating/manufacturing/constructing
engineering/making/producing/effecting
imposing/intruding/invading/impeding
interfering/interposing/interloping/intervening
controlling/managing/directing/steering
manipulating/forcing/coercing/compelling
striving/struggling/efforting/stressing
conflicting/countering/competing/contending
aims/goals/objectives/ends/purposes
effects/results/outcomes/products

EXPERIENCE 46

ENOUGH IS ENOUGH

When Tao is present in our world
Race horses are working in fields
When Tao is not present in our world
War horses are breeding at shrines

No misfortune is greater
Than wanting what others have
No disaster is greater
Than wanting to have more
No calamity is greater
Than not having enough

Being content with what one has
Knowing that enough is enough
Is constantly having enough

Synopsis 46 ❖ Enough is Enough

The presence of Tao in our consciousness and world is being sufficient enough to be sustaining life, preserving Sacredness and eliminating war. There is no greater human tragedy than wanting what others have, wanting more and not having enough; feeling deficient and insufficient and fighting and warring over it. Such envious coveting, greedy desiring and needy lacking are eclipsing and displacing the natural sufficiency of Tao and our innermost, deepest, centermost, truest and utmost Tao-nature by wanting and seeking nonessential external objects and things. Experiencing that who we are and what we already have are enough is true contentment in the sufficiency of Tao, of just what is in our lives and of the reality of our life itself; our most priceless commodity, valuable possession and precious treasure.

Commentary 46 ❖ Enough is Enough

Wise attenders are:

Consciously presencing Tao in the attending relationship/process and are not making hasty interpretations and speedy interventions or engaging in power struggles and interpersonal conflicts that are devastating and destroying its Sacredness.

Having enough referrals, successes, status and income; are not envying the professional practices of colleagues; are working with human beings who are having enough insights, catharses, breakthroughs and transformations and are not being needy or greedy with respect to their progress.

Experiencing that real and true sufficiency are not existing in the material world but, rather, in the Spiritual reality and truth of Tao; the unending and inexhaustible source of abundant wealth, true prosperity, lasting security and complete contentment and are being grateful for the precious gift of human life and being and the spacious opportunity to be attending, encouraging, supporting, assisting, facilitating, guiding, serving and benefiting human beings.

EXPERIENCE 47

AT HOME WITH TAO

Without stepping out of doors
We are understanding our whole world
Without looking out of windows
We are comprehending Heaven's Tao

The farther we are going
The less we are knowing

As wise human beings, we are:
Knowing without going
Seeing without looking
Finding without seeking
Completing without doing

Synopsis 47 ❖ At Home with Tao

Cultivating, internalizing, assimilating, embodying, personifyinng, enacting and identifying *as* Tao are an inner journeying into the deep Core of our Self and Being and the open Heart of our Soul and Spirit. It is not an outward excursion of seeking objects, knowing entities and doing things in the external world. Without leaving our Home of Tao, we can be experiencing, comprehending and understanding the essential reality and nature of Heaven-Earth and the whole world and be discovering and fulfilling our inner Tao-Selves.

Commentary 47 ❖ At Home with Tao.

Wise attenders are:

Able to be understanding worldly taos and comprehending Heavenly Tao through the microcosmic-macrocosmic correspondences (as above/within, so below/without) between the 10,000 things/Wan Wu, Earth, the atomic body, visceral organs, human temperments and outer appearances and Tao, Heaven, the cosmic Spirit, planets, divine Goddesses and inner experiencing.[28]

Experiencing sharing the same One origin, Tao-nature and essential identity as all human beings and, by experiencing themselves inwardly, are able to empathically understand them universally, how we are the same in uniquely different ways and uniquely different in the same way.

Conducting the attending relationship/process in a meditative way; via visualizing, concentrating, reflecting, contemplating and absorbing that is assisting and facilitating human beings in discovering and experiencing their inward focus, inner contact and internal connection; instinctual knowing and intuitive wisdom and interior reality, inherent being and intrinsic nature rather than by going looking and doing seeking in the outer world of external objects, exterior things and outward appearances.

EXPERIENCE 48

NON-INCREASING, NON-INTERFERING

Pursuing knowledge is increasing daily
Cultivating Tao is decreasing daily
Simplifying and simplifying
Again and again
Until we are reaching Non-Doing

Non-Doing
Yet nothing is being left undone

Our world is being gained
By non-interfering
When we are interfering
Our world is being lost

SYNOPSIS 48 ❖ NON-INCREASING, NON-INTERFERING

Knowledge is being pursued by daily increasing. Tao is being cultivated through daily decreasing, simplifying and Non-Doing/No-'thing'-doing/No-Thing doing and our world is being gained, enacted and completed by non-interfering.

COMMENTARY 48 ❖ NON-INCREASING, NON-INTERFERING

Wise attenders are:

Not only pursuing and gaining increased factual information, data and knowledge about human beings through behavioral observations, intake interviewing and history taking; but are cultivating Tao by decreasing and simplifying diagnostic assessing, case formulating and intervention strategizing until Non-Doing/Wu Wei is being reached and space is opening up for the natural activities of human beings to immediately, innocently and freshly generate 'material'.

Experiencing that, when little is being done in the way of using techniques and interventions, the attending relationship/process is naturally proceeding, unfolding, progressing and developing in the way that it is being and doing.

Not interfering with the natural course of the attending relationship/process, Yin/Yang Ch'i alternating dynamics and Wu Wei Ch'i flowing kinetics by purposely planning, devising and implementing interposing theories and intervening methods and are maintaining an emptiness, openness and spaciousness that is allowing its unique ongoing activities to run their course and complete themselves.

EXPERIENCE 49

HEART-MINDS

As wise human beings, we are:
Having no fixed heart-minds
And reflecting the heart-minds of people

We are:
Being good with the good
Being good with the not-good
Such is the goodness of our Virtuosity

We are:
Being trusting with the trustworthy
Being trusting with the untrustworthy
Such is the trustingness of our Virtuosity

As wise human beings, we are:
Living in our one human world
And harmoniously uniting
The heart-minds of people
People are looking and listening attentively
As wise human beings, we are:
Regarding them as our own children

Synopsis 49 ❖ Heart-Minds

Wise human beings are not being subjective and dogmatic and are reflecting the heart-minds of people. They are regarding all people with equality and impartiality and are relating to them with the goodness and trustingness of their Virtuosity/Te, whether or not the people are themselves being good and trustworthy. Wise human beings are living in the human world and are harmoniously uniting with the heart-minds of people who are then being magnetically and attentively attracted to them. Wise human beings, in turn, are regarding people with uncondition*ed* parental love.[29]

Commentary 49 ❖ Heart-Minds

Wise attenders are:

Adopting a phenomenological approach to human beings by suspending and bracketing out theoretical preconceptions, past clinical experience, assumptions about similar 'cases' and expectations for treatment and are not only making definite diagnostic assessments, case formulations, treatment plans, intervention strategies and outcome prognoses.

Openly receiving, clearly reflecting and appropriately responding to the 'givenness' of human beings and whatever is presencing itself and the ways it is happening in the attending relationship/process purely and simply with the goodness and trustingness of their Virtuosity/Te.

Empathizing with, mirroring and reflecting and identifying with the heart-minds of human beings with nonjudgmental equality and impartiality; are staying within their subjective frames of reference and personal worlds of lived experience; are harmoniously synchronizing with their energetic vibrational frequencies and are relating to them with uncondition*ed* parent-like love.[30]

EXPERIENCE 50

ONE OUT OF TEN

As people, we are:
Coming out at birth
Going in at death

Three out of ten of us are each:
Identifying with living
Identifying with dying
Moving between living and dying

How is this so?
Because of our attaching to
Because of our striving for
Life

One out of ten of us is:
Cultivating living very well
And not encountering
Rhinos or tigers on roads
Soldiers or weapons in wars
Having no place within for
Horns of rhinos
Claws of tigers
Swords of soldiers

How is this so?
Because within us
There is no place for dying

Synopsis 50 ❖ One Out of Ten

Nine out of ten people are identifying with either or both living and dying in the life cycle due to varying attachments to and strivings for life and fears and abhorence of death. One out of ten human beings is living beyond dualistic distinctions and identifications of living or dying. Human beings who are truly cultivating and practicing Tao are having no place in their nondual consciousness for dying and, so, are being immune and invulnerable to harm, injury, attack and wounding.

Commentary 50 ❖ One Out of Ten

Wise attenders are:

Identifying *as* nondual Tao's agency in the life cycle of the attending relationship/process and are being free of investments in and attachments to its initiating, strivings for its viability and fears and worries about its terminating.

Experiencing that cultivating and identifying with living are creating an immunity and invulnerability to being harmed, injured, attacked and wounded by human beings in their lives as well as in the attending relationship/process because of having no place in their nondual consciousness for dying.

Deeply and fully committed to living beyond the joys of living and the fears of dying, are living lives of vitality and longevity rather than morbidity and mortality and are modeling the actual ongoing process of living without trying to attain 'life' or to resist living out of fears of either dying or of living deeply, openly, freely and fully.

EXPERIENCE 51

TAO BIRTHING, VIRTUOSITY NOURISHING

Tao is birthing all beings
Virtuosity is nourishing all beings
Matter is forming all beings
Circumstance is completing all beings

So, all beings are:
Honoring Tao, cherishing Virtuosity
Constantly, naturally
Without anyone commanding

Tao is birthing all beings
Virtuosity is nourishing all beings
Protecting and comforting
Supporting and sustaining
Fostering and developing

So, we are:
Originating without possessing
Assisting without controlling
Guiding without forcing

This is Profound Virtuosity

SYNOPSIS 51 ❖ TAO BIRTHING, VIRTUOSITY NOURISHING

That Tao is originating all beings and its Virtuosity/Te is nourishing them are a reality naturally honored and cherished in/*as* the Mysterious originating, Miraculous forming, Marvelous manifesting and Magnificent completing of all beings. Tao and its Virtuosity/Te are protecting, comforting, supporting, sustaining, fostering and developing all beings. Wise human beings, identifying *as* Tao and its Virtuosity/Te, are co-creating, assisting and guiding the material circumstances that are facilitating human beings in forming and completing themselves through the potency and efficacy of profound Virtuosity/Te without possessing, controlling, forcing or dominating them.

COMMENTARY 51 ❖ TAO BIRTHING, VIRTUOSITY NOURISHING

Wise attenders are:

Experiencing that Tao and Virtuosity/Te are originating and developing human beings and all of the rich and varied experiences that are forming and completing themselves in the physical situation and material circumstances of the attending relationship/process.

Naturally and constantly honoring Tao and cherishing Virtuosity/Te as the real originating source and true nourishing re-source that are protecting, comforting, supporting, sustaining, fostering and developing human beings in and throughout the attending relationship/process.

Providing safe, stable and secure conditions, circumstances and relationships for human beings in the attending relationship/process; are co-creating experiences without possessing human beings and are assisting and guiding the attending process through the potentiating efficacy of their profound Virtuosity/Te without controlling, directing or forcing it, or otherwise interfering with or manipulating it.[31]

EXPERIENCE 52

ROOTING AND BRANCHING

Our world has a beginning
Which is being called Mother
Understanding Mother
Is understanding Her offspring
Understanding Her progeny
And still embracing Mother
Is being free from endangering
Throughout our whole lifetime

When we are:
Sealing the openings
Closing the gateways
To the ending of living
We are not endangering

When we are:
Opening the passages
Meddling with events
To the ending of living
We are not completing

Perceiving subtleness is illuminating
Embodying tenderness is strengthening
Utilizing our outer radiating
And returning to inner illuminating
We are not endangering living

This is according with the Constant

SYNOPSIS 52 ❖ ROOTING AND BRANCHING

Understanding Mother Tao as the One origin and Root-Source of our world and understanding Her offspring as the branching of Heaven, Earth, human beings and all beings are not endangering ourselves and other beings. Closing off openings to sensory stimulation is preventing the dissipating, draining, wasting, depleting and losing of life energy/Ch'i and endangering health, vitality, immunity, invulnerability and longevity. Doing so is reserving vitality/Ching, conserving energy/Ch'i and preserving Spirit/Shen and is allowing the continuing developing and completing of oneself and one's living. Perceiving subtleness and embodying softness are illuminating and strengthening and, along with returning to the Inner Light and according with the Constancy of Tao, are preventing the endangering of oneself and one's life and the selves and lives of other human beings.

COMMENTARY 52 ❖ ROOTING AND BRANCHING

Wise attenders are:

Understanding that the real origin of human beings is beginning long before their personal history, the etiology of their difficulties, the onset of their presenting issues or the initiation of the attending relationship/process and that all of its rich and varied experiential phenomena are branching progeny and offsprings of the Root-Source of Mother Tao.

Not losing energy and burning out by opening to overstimulating content and behavior; by making uneconomical and wasteful interventions; by interfering with the natural course of process and by not being Spiritually grounded, centered and contained and, so, are not endangering themselves and human beings or derailing the successful conducting and completing of the attending relationship/process.

Experiencing that perceiving subtleness, e.g., nuances, nonverbal cues and body language, and embodying tenderness, e.g., soft verbalizing, gentle interacting and flexible intervening, in the attending relationship/process are illuminating and strengthening its inner dimensions through the intuitive awarenesses and intersubjective connectedness that accompany according with the Constancy of Tao.

EXPERIENCE **53**

GREAT PATHWAY

Having the least bit of wisdom
I am traveling Great Pathway
Fearing only deviating

Great Pathway is very straight
Yet people are taking detours

Courts are being overdecorated
Grounds are being uncultivated
Storehouses are being depleted

Elegant clothes are being paraded
Ornate weapons are being displayed
Fancy delicacies are being devoured
Surplus riches are being hoarded

All this is vanity and thievery
Certainly not cultivating Tao

SYNOPSIS 53 ❖ GREAT PATHWAY

Wise human beings are not deviating from wayfaring on the Great Pathway of Tao by distractions, diversions and detours. The Great Pathway is straight but people are fond of taking by-paths, side-tracks and short-cuts along the way. Forgetting Tao and not conserving Ch'i energy because of attaching to and indulging in the excessive acquiring and displaying of external objects are ignoring the true reality of Tao and squandering the vital energy/Ch'i and efficacious potency of Virtuosity/Te. Such vanity and robbery is not cultivating Tao.[32]

COMMENTARY 53 ❖ GREAT PATHWAY

Wise attenders are:

Not unwisely going off-course; taking side-tracks, by-paths and short-cuts and making detours because of the alluring presentations, fascinating histories, captivating narratives, seductive experiences, bizarre fantasies, exotic dreams, compelling associations, strange energies, psychic phenomena, etc. of human beings.

Nonetheless, considering that these apparently far-out, out of the way and in the way phenomena are *also* manifestations of Tao that need not be distracting diversions or deviating detours in the attending relationship/process.[33]

Not ignorantly neglecting the ground of Tao, vainly embellishing the context of Tao and robbing the energetic/Ch'i reserves of Virtuosity/Te by displaying elegant theories, indulging in inflated interpretations, parading ornate techniques, making fancy interventions and hoarding financial gains in the attending relationship/process.

EXPERIENCE 54

CULTIVATING VIRTUOSITY

Well founded Tao
Cannot be uprooted
Well enfolded Tao
Cannot be removed

Generation after generation
Is continuing this Holy-making

Cultivating its Virtuosity:
In ourselves is embodying Virtuosity
In our families is compounding Virtuosity
In our communities is enduring Virtuosity
In our countries is abounding Virtuosity
In our worlds is pervading Virtuosity

Therefore, we are contemplating:
Selves in light of ourselves
Families in light of our families
Communities in light of our communities
Countries in light of our countries
Worlds in light of our worlds

How am I knowing that
This is so in our world?
Through and as 'This'

SYNOPSIS 54 ❖ CULTIVATING VIRTUOSITY

Well founded and well contained Tao are the fundamental ground, encompassing space and central Heart of human being that cannot be disconnected, removed or divided and which have been continuously transmitted generation after generation. As the Virtuosity/Te of Tao is being cultivated by human beings; its embodying, compounding, enduring, abounding and pervading goodness, potency and efficacy are radially expanding to their families, communities, countries and worlds. Every living being is being experienced in terms of its absolutely unique individuality, intrinsic nature and inherent integrity, that by which it is being who and what it is in the interconnected web and interdependent network of all living beings. Knowing that this is so in our world is occurring through our identifying *as* Tao and its Virtuosity/Te in the here-now present moment of the vast panorama of being and living, all 'This', All That Is As It Is without and within ourselves.

COMMENTARY 54 ❖ CULTIVATING VIRTUOSITY

Wise attenders are:

Experiencing Tao *as* the fundamental ground, encompassing context and central Heart of their being and that of other human beings that are remaining firmly rooting, solidly containing and deeply connecting throughout the attending relationship/process.

Embodying and cultivating the radiating light of Tao and energy/ Ch'i of Virtuosity/Te and are experiencing that their compounding, enduring, abounding and pervading are universally in-fluencing (in-flowing) human beings and their families, communities, countries and worlds.

Regarding individual human beings and their radially expanding relationships as universally shared embodiments and personifications of the multiplicity, diversity, unity, identity and totality of Tao and its interconnected web and interdependent network, the here-now 'This' of All That Is As It Is in the outer world and inner experiencing.

TZU

SELF
I/ME/MY/PERSONAL
NATURAL/SPONTANEOUS

JAN

SO/THUS/LIKE THIS
YES/CERTAINLY/REALLY
RIGHT

NATURAL/SPONTANEOUS/SELF-LIKE/SELF-SO PRESENCING,
APPEARING AND MANIFESTING OF ANY/ALL EXPERIENTIAL
PHENOMENA WITHIN CONSCIOUSNESS AND AWARENESS.

OF/BY/AS-ITSELF-SO
AS-SUCH/JUST-SO/AS-IS
WHAT-IS/WHAT-IS-SO
UNDERIVED/UNCONDITIONED
UNPLANNED/UNINTENDED
UNREPEATED/UNREPLAYED
UNREHEARSED/UNPERFORMED
IMPROVISED/AD LIB/IMPROMPTU
UNREPRODUCED/UNREPLICATED
SERENDIPITOUS/HAPPENING
SUI GENERIS/DE NOVO/ORIGINAL
IN VIVO/IN SITU/PRESENCING
CONCRETE/DIRECT/IMMEDIATE
NATURE/FREEDOM

EXPERIENCE 55

PERFECT HARMONY

Embodying abundant Virtuosity
We are resembling an infant child

Poisonous insects are not stinging us
Wild animals are not attacking us
Predatory birds are not striking us

Our bones are flexible
Our muscles are pliable
Yet our grasp is strong

Not yet knowing the relating
Of females and males
Our life force is perfect

Crying all day without becoming hoarse
Our natural harmony is perfect

Being harmonious is according with the Constant
According with the Constant is being illuminated

Forcing the growing of life is ominous
Using our heart-mind
For manipulating our vital energy is powerful
But overdeveloping power is accelerating decay
This is not according with Tao
Whatever is not following Tao
Is quickly coming to an early ending

Synopsis 55 ❖ Perfect Harmony

Embodying abundant Virtuosity/Te is returning to the primordial energy/Yuan Ch'i, original vitality, tender flexibility and natural harmony of an infant child that is resulting in safety, security, immunity and invulnerability to harm and injury.[34] Being harmonious is according with Constant Tao and is being illuminating. Forcing growing and developing, especially by using heart-mind for manipulating and potentiating vital energy/Ch'i, is interfering with the natural alternating, balancing and reversing of Tao's Yin/Yang Ch'i dynamics and the flowing, circulating and returning of Wu Wei Ch'i kinetics and is accelerating degeneration, deterioration, decay and death. This is not according with and following Tao, is being contrary to the natural developmental and organic evolutional process of Tao and is rapidly leading to, and eventuating in, premature endings and not reaching Tao.[35/36]

Commentary 55 ❖ Perfect Harmony

Wise attenders are:

Embodying abundant Virtuosity/Te; are experiencing infant child-like original immunity, vital energy, tender strength and natural harmony by being in accord with and following Constant Tao and being illuminated by its Inner Light and are creating a safe, secure and nonthreatening attending relationship/process for human beings.

Not forcing the growing and developing of human beings or the progressing and completing of the attending relationship/process by making intense interactions and confrontations or using catalytic techniques and procedures that are radically interfering with the natural dynamic alternating and kinetic flowing of their proceeding, unfolding and completing.

Experiencing that overdeveloping power and using it to manipulate vital energy, force changes and accelerate growth are not in accord with or following Tao; are only creating defensiveness, resistance, reactivity, power struggles and acting-out in human beings; are violating the natural integrity and organic harmony of the attending relationship/process and are rapidly bringing about its early termination.

EXPERIENCE 56

PROFOUNDLY IDENTIFYING

Understanding, we are not necessarily speaking
Speaking, we are not necessarily understanding

We are:
Sealing the openings
Closing the gateways
Smoothing sharp edges
Loosening tight knots
Softening bright lights
Settling dusty worlds
This is Profoundly Identifying

When we are profoundly identifying
It is impossible to be:
Intimate or indifferent with us
Helpful or harmful to us
Commending or condemning of us

As such, we are being
The greatest treasure
Of our whole world

SYNOPSIS 56 ❖ PROFOUNDLY IDENTIFYING

Wise human beings are not usually or necessarily saying much about their inner understandings of the essential realities and truths of Tao, Nature, Heaven-Earth, the multiverse and cosmos and the world and human beings. Profoundly identifying *as* Tao and Virtuosity/Te are involving being inwardly self-contained and closing off excessive sensory input and are allowing the natural compensating and counterbalancing of experiences to be occurring, e.g., smoothing sharp edges, loosening tight knots, softening bright lights and settling dusty worlds. Profoundly Tao-identifying human beings are living beyond positive-negative bipolarities such as intimacy/indifference, helpfulness/harmfulness and commendation/condemnation and are being our whole world's greatest gift and most precious treasure.

COMMENTARY 56 ❖ PROFOUNDLY IDENTIFYING

Wise attenders are:

Not intellectualizing and necessarily speaking with human beings about ineffable Tao; the potency and efficacy of Virtuosity/Te; the workings of Yin/Yang Ch'i dynamics and Wu Wei Ch'i kinetics; the Mystery of origination, the Miracles of formation, the Marvels of manifestation and the Magnificence of completion and are not wastefully outflowing vital energy/Ch'i.

Further conserving the vital energy/Ch'i and efficacious potency of their Virtuosity/Te by not opening to external sensory input and are allowing the natural compensating and counterbalancing dynamics of Yin/Yang Ch'i energies to be soothing the pains, relaxing the tensions, softening the intensities and settling the confusions of human beings in the attending relationship/process.

Profoundly identifying *as* nondual Tao and its Virtuosity/Te, are living beyond many dualistic positive/negative distinctions in the feelings, relationships, behaviors, activities and judgments of human beings and, as such, are being greatly treasured in the attending relationship/process.

EXPERIENCE 57

GOVERNING BY TAO

We are governing this State straightforwardly
We are deploying armies strategically
We are gaining our world by not interfering
How am I knowing this is so?
Through and as 'This'

More restrictions and prohibitions
More impoverished people
More machines and weapons
More disordered countries
More cleverness and craftiness
More artificial contrivances
More regulations and ordinances
More criminal activities

As wise human beings:
When we are not forcing
People are transforming of themselves so
When we are not controlling
People are regulating of themselves so
When we are not interfering
People are prospering of themselves so
When we are not desiring
People are simplifying of themselves so

Synopsis 57 ❖ Governing by Tao

Wise human beings, through the inner reality of their actual living experience, are understanding that governing by Tao is not strategizing about or interfering with the natural course of people's lives or of unfolding events. The more ordinances, prohibitions, weapons and craftiness there are; the more people are becoming indigents, outlaws, renegades, criminals, fugitives and refugees. Wise human beings governing by Tao are not controlling or forcing people and are not interfering with or complicating their lives, thus enabling them to be naturally transforming, self-regulating, prospering and simplifying of themselves so/Tzu Jan.

Commentary 57 ❖ Governing by Tao

Wise attenders are:

Conducting the attending relationship/process in a straightforward humanistic manner by being open, clear, direct, disclosing and educative and not in a strategic militaristic manner by being guarded, concealed, covert, tactical and pre-emptive.

Experiencing that the more clever rituals and crafty techniques, the more the attending relationship/process is being contrived and disordered and the more rigid rules and restrictive roles, the more human beings are being impoverished and rebellious.

Experiencing that by not controlling and forcing human beings and by not interfering with and complicating their lives, they are naturally self-regulating, transforming, prospering and simplifying on their own, of themselves so/Tzu Jan.

EXPERIENCE 58

TWO WAYS OF GOVERNING

When our governing is being subdued and unobtrusive
People are being pure and simple
When our governing is being intrusive and invasive
People are being broken and needy

Good fortune is resting upon bad fortune
Bad fortune is residing in good fortune
Who is knowing how and when it will be ending?
Is there neither right nor wrong?
Right is turning into wrong
Wrong is turning into right
Long have people been bewildered

As wise human beings, we are:
Upright, yet not overbearing
Straightforward, yet not overextending
Sharp, yet not piercing
Bright, yet not dazzling

SYNOPSIS 58 ❖ TWO WAYS OF GOVERNING

Subdued and unobtrusive governing are preserving people's purity and simplicity and intrusive and invasive governing are resulting in their brokenness and neediness. What is judged to be good and bad and what is deemed to be right and wrong are continually turning into each other with a confusing lack of apparent standards, norms and constancy. Wise human beings are being sharp and straightforward but not incisive or invasive, upright and bright but not overshadowing or overwhelming.

COMMENTARY 58 ❖ TWO WAYS OF GOVERNING

Wise attenders are:

Characteristically being subdued, unobtrusive, low-key, low-profile, moderate and minimalist in conducting the attending relationship/process, e.g., making fewer objectifying verbalizations, interpretations and interventions, and human beings are feeling more whole and being more genuine.

Assisting human beings in understanding and experiencing apparent dualities as counterbalancing bipolar complements that are continually alternating, reciprocating and reversing and are positively reframing their unwelcomed conditions without rationalizing or negating them, e.g., experiencing symptoms and crises as wake-up calls and growthful opportunities.

Being upright and honest, straightforward and direct, sharp and to the point and bright and illuminating in conducting the attending relationship/process without being dominating or ignoring the boundaries, disregarding the limits, dishonoring the dignity or violating the integrity of human beings by being incisive, invasive, overshadowing and overwhelming.

EXPERIENCE 59

CONSERVING AND COMPOUNDING

In serving Heaven and governing people
Nothing is surpassing being sparing
Being sparing is recovering early
Recovering early is compounding Virtuosity

Compounding Virtuosity is overcoming anything
Overcoming anything is having unlimited capacity
Having unlimited capacity is governing any state

Being the Mother of this State
Is being long lasting
Having deep roots and solid trunks
The way of long life and enduring vision

Synopsis 59 ❖ Conserving and Compounding

In serving Heavenly Tao and governing people; being frugal, economical and moderate are recovering early through reserving vitality, conserving energy, preserving Spirit and compounding Virtuosity/Te. Compounding Virtuosity/Te is overcoming anything, having unlimited capacity and being able to govern any state of being. Being the Mother Tao State is being deeply rooted and grounded, solidly connected and centered and far-reaching and long-lasting.

Commentary 59 ❖ Conserving and Compounding

Wise attenders are:

Serving and assisting human beings in the attending relationship/ process by not overdoing interventions; by stopping in time, yielding to process and shifting early which is not wasting but recovering, accumulating and compounding the vital energy/Ch'i and efficacious potency of Virtuosity/Te and is increasing the capacity to be efficiently and effectively regulating the experiences of human beings.

Conducting the attending relationship/process in an effortless and frictionless way by not resisting the resistances of human beings or going against the grain and flow of experiences and are having an available reservoir of resourceful healing and transformative energy powerful enough to effect spontaneous remissions in psychosomatic symptoms, psychiatric conditions and physical illnesses.[37]

Being deeply rooted in, and solidly connected with, Mother Tao *as* the real Origin and true Source of the attending relationship/process of human beings which is opening the far-reaching vistas and enabling the long-lasting enduring of their life experiences by seeing them through immanently and/or seeing through them transcendentally.

EXPERIENCE 60

COOKING SMALL FISHES

We are governing a great State
As if cooking small fishes

When we are governing our world with Tao
Phantoms are losing their power
Not only are phantoms losing their power
But their power is not hindering us
Not only is their power not hindering us
But sages, also, are not hindering us

When both are not hindering us
Virtuosity is uniting in both
Accumulating and returning

SYNOPSIS 60 ❖ COOKING SMALL FISHES

Governing by Tao is being delicate, gentle and slow; like cooking small fishes. When the virtual reality of disincarnate phantoms[38] and the real virtuality of embodied sages are both being integrated into the energy and power of true Virtuosity; it is accumulating in both, not hindering the developing of human beings and is returning them to Tao.

COMMENTARY 60 ❖ COOKING SMALL FISHES

Wise attenders are:

Conducting and regulating the attending relationship/process consciously, attentively, carefully, gently and delicately with minimal flipping and poking.

Assisting human beings in not hindering developing their unique identities by identifying with the supernatural powers of either intro-jections of disembodied psychic entities or projections onto embodied holy beings.

Experiencing that when both phantom introjections and sagely projections are being withdrawn and their powers defused; human beings are opening to and accumulating the energy and potency of true Virtuosity/Te and are returning to their original Tao-nature.

EXPERIENCE 61

CONVERGING POINTS

Developed states are being like river deltas
They are converging points of our world
They are being the feminine of our world
Feminine is constantly overcoming masculine
By naturally being low, deep and still

Developed states are receiving undeveloped ones
By lowering themselves before them
Undeveloped states are receiving developed ones
By lowering themselves before them
The former are receiving by consciously lowering
The latter are receiving by naturally being lower

Developed states are wanting to include and provide
Undeveloped states are wanting to join and serve
Both states are each obtaining what they want
By developed states lowering themselves

Synopsis 61 ❖ Converging Points

Developed states, by intentionlly lowering themselves, and undeveloped states, by naturally being lower, are being receptive places of convergence and confluence. Both are having a mutual interest in uniting with each other. Developed states are wanting to annex, incorporate and provide for undeveloped ones. Undeveloped states are wanting to affiliate, join and serve developed ones. By intentionally being lower than undeveloped states, developed states are creating a positive in-fluence (in-flowing) upon undeveloped states and an integrative con-fluence (flowing-with) of the two states.

Commentary 61 ❖ Converging Points

Wise attenders are:

Identifying *as* the developed State of Tao and its Yin dimension that is being low, deep, still, magnetically attracting and centripetally receiving and are creating a place of in-fluence, convergence and con-fluence for the experiences of human beings in the attending relationship/process.

Supporting, assisting, facilitating and guiding human beings in experiencing and integrating undeveloped ego-states and developed Tao-States in their intrapsychic and interpersonal relationships.

Being humbly occupying a phenomenological interpersonal space below that of human beings, providing them with inclusive support and affording them the opportunity to participate in the attending relationship/process.

EXPERIENCE **62**

WORLD'S GREATEST TREASURE

Tao is being the sanctuary of all beings
As developed human beings
It is our perfection
As undeveloped people
It is our protection

Fine words are buying favor
Good deeds are winning over
Yet, even if we are not developing
Tao is still not abandoning us

At the installing of emperors
At the appointing of ministers
Presenting jade discs and horse teams
Does not equal sitting still
And offering Tao

As Ancient Ones:
Why are we so treasuring Tao?
Because seeking Tao, we are coming to Tao
Because not seeking Tao, Tao is coming to us
Thus, Tao is being our world's greatest treasure

SYNOPSIS 62 ❖ WORLD'S GREATEST TREASURE

Tao is being the subtle inner secret in the Heart of all beings. It is the Spiritual sanctuary and refuge for human beings and is not abandoning any of us, regardless of the degree or extent of our development. Tao is being our world's greatest and most precious treasure and our most worthwhile and valuable offering beyond any and all fine words, good deeds, gifts and wealth. Tao is being treasured from ancient times until the present because seeking Tao, we are coming to Tao and not seeking Tao, Tao is coming to us. Becoming One with/ *as* Tao is inevitable and just a matter of time whether we are knowing it or not.

COMMENTARY 62 ❖ WORLD'S GREATEST TREASURE

Wise attenders are:

Experiencing that Tao is a sanctuary for all human beings, our protection and perfection, and is creating safe guarding and secure guiding in the attending relationship/process.

Experiencing that fine words said and good deeds done in the attending relationship/process may be resulting in positive rapport, therapeutic alliances and collaborative relationships with human beings but that it is Tao that is providing a safe and secure crucible in which to explore and transform unfortunate and painful life-experiences, e.g., early trauma, physical violence, sexual abuse, neglect, shaming, invalidation, abandonment, etc..

Experiencing Tao *as* their greatest blessing, gift and treasure in conducting the attending relationship/process because Tao's Virtuosity/Te is being found by human beings who are conscious of it and is finding human beings who are not conscious of it, since nothing is separate from Tao except in the conditioned and limited ego-minds of human beings.

EXPERIENCE 63

SUBTLE DOINGS

We are:
Acting without forcing
Serving without managing
Tasting without savoring

We are:
Making great things small
Making many things few
Repaying hurt with Virtuosity

We are:
Addressing difficult issues early
While they are still being easy
Addressing great matters early
While they are still being small

Difficult issues are beginning with easy ones
Great matters are beginning with small ones

As wise human beings:
We are not striving for greatness
Yet are often attaining greatness

Making promises lightly
Is lacking in trust and faith
And resulting in great difficulties

As wise human beings:
We are considering everything difficult
And, in the end, are having no difficulty

SYNOPSIS 63 ❖ SUBTLE DOINGS

Wise human beings are acting, serving and experiencing without forcing, managing and savoring. They are regarding the great as small, the many as few and are repaying hurt with the goodness, kindness, forgiveness and gratitude of their Virtuosity/Te. Wise human beings are addressing and dealing with great matters and difficult issues early while they are still being small and easy. They are not striving for greatness yet are often accomplishing great things. When wise human beings are regarding the easy as hard, the hard is becoming easy. They are not making easy promises that are lacking in truth and are resulting in distrust and great difficulties; are considering the difficulties in everything and, in the end, are having no difficulties.

COMMENTARY 63 ❖ SUBTLE DOINGS

Wise attenders are:

Acting without forcing, serving without managing and experiencing without savoring and are allowing and following the Wu Wei Ch'i activities that are naturally, frictionlessly, effortlessly and seamlessly flowing from their awarenesses and those of human beings in the attending relationship/process.

Simplifying the attending relationship/process by reducing the magnitude and complexity of issues by distilling them down to their essential nature, by attending to warning lights on the dashboard of process and by addressing issues early while they may be smaller and easier to be making self-corrective in-flight modifications and short-circuiting the cascading of ignored emotions and suppressed behaviors.[39]

Not striving for great accomplishments or quick and easy fixes in the attending relationship/process, are not minimizing its difficulties or making incredible promises about its successful progression and are experiencing that, nonetheless, clear awarenesses, deep connections, profound insights, radical breakthroughs and lasting transformations are occurring easily.

WAN	WU
萬	物

10,000/MYRIAD/MANY	THINGS/BEINGS/ENTITIES
INDEFINITE NUMBER	MATTER/SUBSTANCE
INNUMERABLE	MATERIAL/ARTICLES
COUNTLESS	OUTSIDE MATTERS
ALL	WHOLLY

THE INFINITE MULTIPLICITY/DIVERSE TOTALITY OF EXPERIENTIAL
PHENOMENA WITHIN CONSCIOUSNESS AND AWARENESS.

MULTIPLICITY	OBJECTIFICATIONS
DIVERSITY	EXPERIENCES
COMPLETENESS	PHENOMENA
TOTALITY	IMMANENT TAO

EXPERIENCE 64

STARTING AT THE BEGINNING

What is:
Still is easy to maintain
Subtle is easy to contain
What is:
Frail is easy to shatter
Small is easy to scatter

We are anticipating issues
Before they are coming into being
We are regulating matters
Before they are going out of order

Large trees are growing from tiny shoots
Tall towers are rising from small mounds
Long trips are starting from first steps

Forcing things is ruining them
Seizing things is losing them
As wise human beings, we are:
Forcing nothing and ruining nothing
Seizing nothing and losing nothing

As people, we are often failing
When close to completing
When we are being as attentive
At endings as at beginnings
Nothing is being ruined or lost

As wise human beings, we are:
Desiring to be desireless
Not valuing rare objects
Learning to be unlearned
Returning to what people are disregarding
Assisting all beings to develop naturally
Without ourselves acting unnaturally

SYNOPSIS 64 ❖ STARTING AT THE BEGINNING

Attending to phenomena while they are still, subtle, frail and small is making it easier to contain and to disperse them. Anticipating phenomena before they are coming into being and regulating them before they are going out of order are making it possible to be addressing and handling matters, affairs and issues. All phenomena are growing and developing from small beginnings. Forcing the process and seizing the products of natural developing are ruining and losing the vitality, integrity and viability of being and living. Being attentive throughout the entire developmental process, starting at its beginning and finishing at its ending, is allowing for its successful completing and is preventing its ruin and loss. Wise human beings are not desiring rare objects and erudite knowledge. They are returning to Tao and are assisting all beings in cultivating and developing the simplicity and sufficiency of their original Tao-nature and Virtuosity/Te naturally without interfering or acting unnaturally themselves.

COMMENTARY 64 ❖ STARTING AT THE BEGINNING

Wise attenders are:

Experiencing that usually how the attending relationship/process is beginning is how it is continuing, are practicing early intervention by addressing issues while they are still small and are practicing preventative maintenance by anticipating issues before they are coming into being and regulating matters before they are going out of order.[39]

Not forcing or attaching to the developing of issues in the attending relationship/process, are not risking ruining or losing the experiential phenomena that are spontaneously presencing and unfolding themselves, are being as attentive and careful at the terminating of the attending relationship/process as they were at its initiating and are not risking ruining or losing earlier gains and good closure as it is naturally developing.

Not desiring and valuing particular object-contents or change-forms during the course of the attending relationship/process, are learning to unlearn theories and techniques, are returning to a Tao-centered state of being and are assisting human beings in the natural developing of their unique Tao-nature and Virtuosity/Te without intervening in any unnatural, interfering and inappropriate ways.

EXPERIENCE 65

GOVERNING AND RETURNING

Being Ancient Ones fully identifying as Tao
We are not using it for educating people
But for restoring their simplicity

As people, we are being difficult to govern
Because of being overly sophisticated

Clever governing is robbing this State
Clear governing is blessing this State
Understanding these two matters
We are understanding the Constant Pattern
Constantly embodying this Model
Is Profound Virtuosity

Profound Virtuosity
Is deeply-penetrating and far-reaching
Returning all beings to the Great Accord

Synopsis 65 ❖ Governing and Returning

Identifying *as* Tao is restoring and returning to Primordial Simplicity[40] rather than being too sophisticated. Clever, cunning and crafty governing; using guile and artifice, plots and tricks, are robbing the State of Tao. Clear, open and honest governing are blessing the State of Tao. Understanding this is understanding and embodying the Pattern and Model of Constant Tao and its Profound Virtuosity/Te. Profound Virtuosity/Te is deeply-penetrating and far-reaching and is returning all beings to the Great Accord.

Commentary 65 ❖ Governing and Returning

Wise attenders are:

Fully identifying *as* ancient Tao and are assisting human beings in restoring the primordial simplicity, wholeness and complete harmony of their original Tao-nature and Virtuosity/Te.

Not using clever theories, implementing cunning strategies and employing crafty techniques in the attending relationship/process, e.g., double binds, prescribing symptoms and paradoxical intentions, that are interfering with the naturally developing self-experiencing, self-understanding and self-regulating of human beings due to too much intellectual knowledge and psychological sophistication.

Being clear, open, direct and honest with human beings in the attending relationship/process and are assisting them in restoring the deeply-penetrating and far-reaching power of their Virtuosity/Te, their gift and genius of absolutely unique individuality, and in returning to the complete unity and harmony of their Original Tao-nature, Tao-Being and Tao-Self.

EXPERIENCE 66

SUPPORTING AND BACKING

Great rivers are governing
Hundreds of valley streams
By being below them

As wise human beings:
In some ways being above people
We are conversing from below them
In some ways being ahead of people
We are following from behind them

As wise human beings:
At some times being on top of people
We are not burdening them
At some times being in front of people
We are not obstructing them

Being so, our whole world
Is happily and untiringly upholding us
As wise human beings
We are not contending
And there is no contending

Synopsis 66 ❖ Supporting and Backing

Being lower is naturally governing by receiving the downflowing and inflowing of vital energies and the living process. Wise human beings are supporting and elevating and are backing and advancing people by staying below them and following behind them and by not burdening them from above or obstructing them from ahead. Likewise, wise human beings are being joyfully and untiringly upheld and endorsed by people without any contending.[41]

Commentary 66 ❖ Supporting and Backing

Wise attenders are:

Being like great rivers of Tao receiving the downward and inward streaming of ego-identifying human beings by being low, deep, empty, humble and receptive and due to the effortless downward pull of gravity and the inward draw of the void.

Inhabiting a phenomenological interpersonal space that is staying below and following behind human beings in the attending relationship/process and are supporting and elevating them without burdening them from above and are backing and advancing them without obstructing them from ahead.

Being reciprocally backed and supported by human beings in the attending relationship/process who are continually and happily grateful for being so upheld and uplifted and forwarded and furthered in their cooperative, collaborative, non-competetive and non-contentious relationship.

EXPERIENCE 67

THREE TREASURES OF TAO

Our whole world is saying
Great Tao is seeming like nothing at all
It is just because of this
That it is being so great
That which is seeming like something
Is not being so great

We are having three treasures
Held fast and kept safe
First is uncondition*ed* love
Second is conserved resources
Third is restrained precedence

Unconditioning love, we can be courageous
Conserving resources, we can be generous
Restraining precedence, we can be splendrous

Being courageous without uncondition*ed* love
Being generous without conserved resources
Being splendrous without restrained precedence
Can bring about ruin and death

Through uncondition*ed* loving, we are:
Succeeding in the offensive
Sustaining in the defensive

Heaven is protecting and saving us
Through uncondition*ed* loving

SYNOPSIS 67 ❖ THREE TREASURES OF TAO

The Three Treasures/San Po of Great Tao, being held fast and kept safe by wise human beings; are conserved resources, unconditioned love and restrained precedence[42] that, respectively, are allowing them to be generous, courageous and splendrous. But being the latter, without conserved resources, unconditioned love and restrained precedence can be resulting in ruin and death. Unconditioned loving is being sustaining in the defensive and succeeding in the offensive. The unconditioned loving of Heavenly Tao is safeguarding and rescuing human beings.[43]

COMMENTARY 67 ❖ THREE TREASURES OF TAO

Wise attenders are:

Observing that Great Tao is relatively unknown by professional colleagues and seeming like no-thing at all, that there are many schools in the psychotherapy/counseling world with reductionistic-mechanistic approaches and that, while seeming like something, are not so great.

Having Three Treasures/San Po that they are embodying and safeguarding:

1. Conserving resources and being frugal by making concise interactions and economical interventions that are constituting the abundant reserves enabling them to be generous and not exhausted.

2. Unconditioning love and being compassionate by being non-judgmental and empathically understanding that are constituting the harmonious equality enabling them to be courageous and not endangered.

3. Restraining precedence and being humble by according with experiences and following processes that are constituting the deferent modesty enabling them to be splendrous and not desecrated.

Experiencing that unconditioned loving is enabling them to be impartially, compassionately and successfully conducting and sustaining the attending relationship/process with a wide variety of human beings with a wide variety of psychological conditions and clinical issues and to be efficiently and effectively utilizing a wide variety of treatment modalities in a wide variety of clinical settings, being guarded and guided by Heavenly Tao.

EXPERIENCE 68

NON-CONTENDING, NON-COERCING

As most developed warriors
We are not being hurtful
As most developed fighters
We are not being rageful
As most developed victors
We are not being vengeful
As most developed leaders
We are not being forceful

This is:
The Virtuosity of not contending
The potency of not coercing
Matching the ultimacy of Heaven

SYNOPSIS 68 ❖ NON-CONTENDING, NON-COERCING

Most developed warriors, fighters, victors and leaders are not being hurtful, rageful, vengeful or forceful. They are being non-violent, non-contending and non-coercing and the potency, utility and efficacy of their Virtuosity/Te are matching the ultimacy of Heavenly Tao.

COMMENTARY 68 ❖ NON-CONTENDING, NON-COERCING

Wise attenders are:

Being real and true warriors of the Body, Mind, Heart, Soul and Spirit of Tao and human beings; are engaging in wayfaring and not warfaring in the attending relationship/process and are not fighting defenses and resistances, defeating symptoms and conditions and forcing change and surrender.

Not being forceful, angry, hurtful and rewounding of human beings in the attending relationship/process even when dealing with interpersonal conflicts, power struggles, negative transferences and hostile-aggressive acting-out.

Experiencing that when the potency and efficacy of their Virtuosity/Te are actualized in non-contending and non-coercing, they are matching the ultimacy of Heavenly Tao.

EXPERIENCE 69

NO ENEMIES

As military strategists:
We are not taking the offensive
And are taking the defensive
We are not advancing an inch
And are retreating a foot

This is:
Deploying forces without marching them
Facing opponents without engaging them
Displaying weapons without employing them
Defeating armies without battling them

For us, there is no greater calamity
Than creating and fighting 'enemies'
And losing our treasures

So, when opposing forces are warring
Only uncondition*ed* loving is winning

Synopsis 69 ❖ No Enemies

By strategically taking the defensive and retreating rather than taking the offensive and advancing; deploying forces, facing opponents, displaying weapons and defeating armies are respectively accomplished without marching, engaging, employing or battling them. Wise human beings are not creating and fighting 'enemies'[44] and are not losing the Three Treasures of Tao/San Po, i.e., conserved resources, uncondition*ed* love and restrained precedence. When opposing forces are warring, only uncondition*ed* loving is winning.

Commentary 69 ❖ No Enemies

Wise attenders are:

Not taking an assertive, advancing, confrontational or aggressive approach toward human beings in the attending relationship/process and are typically stepping back, down and aside and allowing it to be proceeding and unfolding naturally and spontaneously without making interfering, intrusive and invasive interventions or pre-emptive strikes and frontal attacks on issues.

Having an available response repertoire and tool kit for assisting human beings in addressing and working on their issues but are not usually using them and, instead, are relying upon the efficacious power of their Virtuosity/Te to naturally potentiate and catalyze the work and to win the day.

Experiencing that there is no greater tragedy than to be creating and engaging human beings as 'others', opponents, adversaries and 'enemies' to fight and defeat and, thus, to be losing the three treasures of Tao by squandering conserved resources, negating uncondition*ed* love and violating restrained precedence in competetive contests, interpersonal conflicts and power struggles.

UNDERSTANDING AND PRACTICING

Understanding my words is very easy
Practicing my works is very easy
Yet, few people in our world
Are understanding and practicing them

My words are having an ancestral source
My works are having a masterful guide
People are not understanding this
So, they are not understanding me

The few who are understanding me
The more they are being empowered

As wise human beings, we are:
Wearing coarse clothes on our bodies
Bearing precious jewels in our hearts

Synopsis 70 ❖ Understanding and Practicing

Understanding and practicing the words and works of Tao are being easy but rare. The ancestral source of Tao and the masterful re-source of Virtuosity/Te are being understood and practiced by only a few human beings. The few human beings who are identifying *as* Tao and its dynamic-kinetic activities are being endowed (en-Tao-ed) and empowered with its uniquely individualizing and personifying Virtuosity/Te. Their ordinary outer appearance is concealing the precious jewel of Tao in their Heart-of-Hearts.[45]

Commentary 70 ❖ Understanding and Practicing

Wise attenders are:

Being a relatively few rarely comprehended professional psychotherapists/counselors who are understanding and practicing the wisdom of the *Tao Te Ching* and bringing it into the attending relationship/process with human beings who are nonetheless being empowered and benefited by them and who are highly regarding and valuing them.

Experiencing that the principles and practices of the attending relationship/process are originating in and being guided by Tao, its Virtuosity/Te, the dynamic-kinetic operating of Yin/Yang Ch'i and Wu Wei Ch'i energies and the natural spontaneity/Tzu Jan that result in the manifesting of all of its diverse experiential phenomena/Wan Wu within their consciousness.

Conducting the attending relationship/process in ways that are outwardly appearing as two human beings who are sitting down engaging in, sharing and enjoying close relating and good conversing; while the precious treasure of Tao is dwelling in/*as* the deep, clear, empty and open center of their Heart-of-Hearts.

EXPERIENCE 71

BEING SICK OF SICKNESS

Understanding and not acting knowing is wellness
Not understanding and acting knowing is sickness

Being sick of this sickness
Is not being sick

As wise human beings:
We are being sick of this sickness
By being sick of this sickness
We are not being sick

Synopsis 71 ❖ Being Sick of Sickness

Wellness is truly understanding and not acting 'knowing' and sickness is not understanding and acting all-knowing. Wise human beings are knowing that they don't know rather than thinking and believing that they know. They are innocently ignoring knowing and wisely knowing ignoring and are ignorantly innocent rather than arrogantly astute. Wise human beings are being sick of the sickness of reducing the Mystery, Miracles, Marvels and Magnificence of human being and living to the conceptual objects of the intellectualized construing, rational thinking and discursive reasoning of the ego-mind.[46]

Commentary 71 ❖ Being Sick of Sickness

Wise attenders are:

Being well-versed in psychotherapy/counseling theories, techniques and methodologies without appearing and acting as pretentious 'know-it-alls' confidently parading limited knowledge as wisdom and game-playing as expertise, especially given the vulnerabilities of human beings and their vital needs for reality, truth, clarity, sanity, honesty and competency in the attending relationship/process.

Not reducing ultimate Spiritual realities to psychological levels of understanding, e.g., the transpersonal dimension of psychology rather than the psychological dimension of the transpersonal; without denying that, in some instances, apparent Spiritual development may be a massive ego-defense against early trauma, abuse and neglect and a flight out of the body into derealized, depersonalized and dissociated states of consciousness.

Deeply appreciating the presence of the Great Mystery, small Miracles, tiny Marvels and Great Magnificence continually occurring in the life of the attending relationship/process and are fully acknowledging the honor, privilege and opportunity of sharing in them with other human beings.

EXPERIENCE 72

RESPECTING THE AWESOME

As people:
When we are not respecting the awesome
The awful is descending upon us

As wise human beings
We are not compressing people's homes
We are not oppressing people's lives
And by not doing so
People are not being suppressed
Repressed and depressed

As wise human beings, we are:
Knowing but not displaying ourselves
Valuing but not glorifying ourselves

Rejecting the outer 'that'
Accepting the inner 'This'

SYNOPSIS 72 ❖ RESPECTING THE AWESOME

Denying, ignoring or disrespecting the awesome are constellating and precipitating the awful in the human Psyche and world. Wise leaders are not narrowing, diminishing, stunting, stifling, blocking, burdening or crushing the lives and selves of fellow human beings that are resulting in their being profoundly disheartened and despirited. Wise leaders are creating conditions for human beings to naturally transition from the awfulness of authoritarian control to the awesomeness of the authoring, authority, authoritativeness and authenticity of their real, true and genuine selves. Wise human beings are understanding and valuing but not displaying or glorifying themselves. They are identifying *as* their innate, inherent and intrinsic Tao-nature and not with externalized others, objects and things in/of the outer world and are accepting the 'This' of internalized Tao, interior Virtuosity/Te and the reality and truth of inner experiencing.

COMMENTARY 72 ❖ RESPECTING THE AWESOME

Wise attenders are:

Respecting the awesome presence of Tao and the power of Virtuosity/Te and the realities of the Mystery of originating, the Miracles of forming, the Marvels of manifesting and the Magnificence of completing and are not constellating and precipitating awful experiences in their consciousness and lives or those of human beings or in the life of the attending relationship/process.

Assisting human beings in working with their traumas, abuses, tragedies and negative experiences and their flashbacks, nightmares, repressed memories and shadow material without using rigid rules, fixed roles and stiff rituals in the attending relationship/process that are constricting and restricting their selves and lives and further oppressing, discouraging, disheartening, demoralizing and despiriting them.

Understanding and valuing themselves but are not displaying or glorifying their gifts, genius, talents and abilities in the conducting of the attending relationship/process and are identifying with/*as* inner realities, truths and beings rather than outer objects, things and 'others'.

SHENG   JEN

SACRED   HUMAN BEING
HOLY/SAINTLY   PERSON/PEOPLE
SAGELY/WISE   HUMANKIND/EVERYONE
DIVINE   POPULACE/MASSES

HUMAN BEINGS WHO STAND ON FIRM GROUND/
LISTEN TO/HEAR/UNDERSTAND/COMPLY WITH/SPEAK
AND ACT FROM WHAT IS GOING ON
IMMEDIATELY/DIRECTLY/CLEARLY/FULLY.

TAO-FOCUSED/CENTERED
TAO-EMBODIED/PERSONIFIED
TAO-REALIZED/ACTUALIZED
TAO-PERFECTED/FULFILLED
TAO-RETURNED/COMPLETED
TAO-IDENTIFIED/TAO-LIKE
NATURAL/UNIVERSAL
ORDINARY/EVERYDAY
BEING-TAO

EXPERIENCE 73

HEAVEN'S NETWORK

Being courageous by daring is risking dying
Being courageous by not daring is preserving living
Of these two, at various times,
One is being gainful
One is being harmful
Who is knowing why Heaven prefers what it does?
Even sages are not always being certain

Heaven's Tao is:
Sustaining without striving
Responding without speaking
Attracting without inviting
Completing without planning

Heaven's network is vast and wide-meshed
Yet nothing and no one are slipping through

SYNOPSIS 73 ❖ HEAVEN'S NETWORK

Being courageous by daring is risking dying and being courageous by not daring is preserving living. What is gainful or harmful in living and dying is sometimes difficult to discern. Heaven's workings are mysterious and inexplicable but inevitable and inexorable. Heavenly Tao is naturally sustaining, responding, attracting and completing without striving, speaking, inviting and planning. Heavenly Tao's network is being vast and wide-meshed yet nothing and no one are being overlooked, missed, ignored, disregarded, forgotten, rejected or lost.

COMMENTARY 73 ❖ HEAVEN'S NETWORK

Wise attenders are:

Being courageous in the attending relationship/process through uncondition*ed* loving, preserving living and respecting dying and are careful when taking risks or making risky interventions that may or may not be helpful and possibly be harmful.

Identifying *as* their Heavenly Tao-nature; are embodying its clearness, emptiness, stillness and oneness in the attending relationship/process; are sustaining it without striving, are responding to human beings without necessarily verbalizing, are attracting material without inviting it and are completing process without planning it.

Identifying *as* the vast and wide-meshed network of Heavenly Tao and the openness, spaciousness, expansiveness and receptiveness of their witness consciousness, free-floating/evenly-hovering attention and observing ego that are not allowing any of the rich and varied experiential phenomena of the attending relationship/process to be slipping through, missed or lost.

EXPERIENCE 74

GREAT EXECUTIONER

As people, if we are not fearing dying
Why be threatening us with death penalties?
As people, even if we are fearing dying
And murderers are being captured
Who is daring to execute them?

Only the Official Executioner is killing killers
Substituting for the Official Executioner
Is like replacing a master carpenter
Taking over for a master carpenter
We are usually injuring our own hands

Synopsis 74 ❖ Great Executioner

What purpose is capital punishment serving if human beings are not fearing dying and, even if we are fearing dying, how can we be justifying killing killers, ourselves destroying the precious blessing and gift of human life? Great Tao is masterfully executing the activities of human beings. It is egotistical, ignorant, arrogant, inflated and grandiose for us to be substituting for or replacing Great Tao's agency in compensating wrongdoing, dispensing punishments and exacting retribution. Even though we are identifying *as* Tao, being so is not being a new and better ego-identity or self-concept, i.e., by 'playing Tao'. If we are not 'getting out of the way' or if we are 'getting in the way' of Great Tao's executing and are taking matters into our own hands, we are usually injuring ourselves.

Commentary 74 ❖ Great Executioner

Wise attenders are:

Not frightening human beings with fatal mortal prospects of chronic mental illness and incapacitating psychiatric disabilities if they are not committing to psychotherapy/counseling and dealing with unforgettable and unforgivable experiences of neglect, abandonment, trauma, abuse, torment, pain, violence and wounding that have scarred their bodies, deranged their minds, damaged their selves, ruined their lives, negated their beings, battered their psyches, disabled their wills, destroyed their worlds, devastated their relationships, crippled their hearts, robbed their Souls and killed their Spirits.

Assisting human beings in holding the perpetrators of the above sufferings accountable without taking revenge; in trusting that Tao, as the Official Executioner, will be 'taking care of' them; and in taking charge of recovering, restoring, reclaiming, reowning and renewing the purity, dignity, integrity, beauty and worthiness of their original inborn Tao-nature, Virtuosity/Te and Human Being.

Not doing the often hard work of/for human beings in the attending relationship/process; are getting out of the way and allowing the dynamic-kinetic operations of Tao to self-correct and self-complete experiences; are not substituting for Tao's agency or human beings' responsibility and are not injuring themselves or human beings in the process.

TREASURING LIVING

As people, we are going hungry
Because, as leaders, we are taxing too much
So, we are starving

As people, we are acting unruly
Because, as leaders, we are controlling too much
So, we are rebelling

As people, we are ignoring mortality
Because, as leaders, we are demanding too much
So, we are toiling

As wise human beings
Rather than busily striving for a life
We are wisely treasuring our living

Synopsis 75 ❖ Treasuring Living

People are going hungry, acting unruly and ignoring mortality when leaders are overtaxing of their wages, overcontrolling of their activities and overdemanding of their lives. As a consequence, the Selves, Souls and Spirits of human beings are withering, suffering and dying. Wise human beings are treasuring, appreciating and enjoying the reality and actuality of sheerly and utterly being and of purely and simply living rather than 'making a living' by striving for some idea, concept, image, fantasy, dream or hope of a 'life' and what it should, could, may, might, would, must or will be.

Commentary 75 ❖ Treasuring Living

Wise attenders are:

Not overtaxing and impoverishing human beings in psychotherapy/counseling with frequent visits and high fees; not overcontrolling and restricting them by rigid rules and stiff rituals and not overdemanding and pressuring them by requirements and expectations, all of which are only resulting in frustration and discouragement, resistance and acting out and stressing and struggling and are leading to empathic failure and early termination.

Not overwhelming human beings in psychotherapy/counseling with excessive assessments and evaluations, formulations and interpretations, agendas and procedures, goals and objectives and strategies and interventions rather than devising and implementing co-created and collaborative ways of proceeding based upon intersubjectivity and dialogue.

Not busily striving for some ideal image, concept, fantasy, dream, wish or hope *about* what the lives of human beings should or could be and, rather, are assisting them in the attending relationship/process in purely and simply treasuring, appreciating and enjoying the sheer and utter reality and actuality of their being and living and the ways in which they are proceeding, unfolding, transforming, developing and progressing.[46]

EXPERIENCE 76

SOFT AND FLUID

At birth, we are being soft and fluid
At death, we are being hard and rigid
Grasses, trees and all living beings
When alive, are being tender and flexible
When dead, are being withered and brittle

Hard and rigid
Are accompanying dying
Soft and fluid
Are accompanying living

So,
Fixed armies will be shattered
Stiff branches will be snapped

Being hard and rigid is least developed
Being soft and fluid is most developed

SYNOPSIS 76 ❖ SOFT AND FLUID

Alive beings are being soft, tender, flexible, fluid and yielding. Dead things are being hard, withered, brittle, rigid and unyielding. Hard and rigid are accompanying dying and soft and fluid are accompanying living. Fixed and stiff things are being easily shattered and snapped. Most developed is being soft and fluid and least developed is being hard and rigid.

COMMENTARY 76 ❖ SOFT AND FLUID

Wise attenders are:

Using soft tones and flexible methods and making gentle interactions and fluid interventions that are sustaining the aliveness, vitality and vibrancy of the attending relationship/process.

Not being bound by rigid rules, fixed ranks, formal roles and stiff rituals that are deadening and devitalizing the attending relationship/process and are breaking off communication, breaking up relationships, breaking down progress and resulting in its withering, shriveling and dry termination.

Experiencing that, when the attending relationship/process is alive, fresh and juicy; flexible, fluid and yielding; creative, inventive and innovative and improvisational, extemporaneous and spontaneous; the rigid defenses, hard resistances, tight controls, stiff behaviors and fixed patterns of human beings are naturally relaxing, softening, loosening, flexing and flowing.

EXPERIENCE 77

HEAVEN'S TAO

Heaven's Tao is like drawing a bow
What is higher is being lowered
What is lower is being raised
What is longer is being shortened
What is shorter is being lengthened

Heaven's Tao is:
Reducing the excessive
Supplementing the insufficient
People's way is:
Diminishing the deficient
Augmenting the superfluous

Who is having sufficient abundance
To be offering our world?
Only human beings embodying Tao

As wise human beings, we are:
Benefiting all without needing gratitude
Completing works without claiming credit
Not desiring to be displaying excellence

Synopsis 77 ❖ Heaven's Tao

Tao, as the reciprocating, alternating and reversing bipolar dynamics of Yin Ch'i/Yang Ch'i energies, is naturally and appropriately compensating the extremes of complementary counterparts. People, instead, are taking more away from the insufficient and adding more to the sufficient. Wise human beings are allowing the fullness of sufficiency to be naturally flowing into the emptiness of insufficiency of human beings and to be restoring harmonious balance. They are benefiting all beings without needing gratitude, claiming credit or displaying excellence.

Commentary 77 ❖ Heaven's Tao

Wise attenders are:

Experiencing the Soul-work of the attending relationship/process as bringing down Heavenly Yang Spiritual energy into physical being, i.e., inSpiriting body (animation) and lifting up Earthly Yin physical energy to Spiritual Being, i.e., embodying Spirit (incorporation); integrating body-Spirit and Spirit-body and preventing their separation into either the horror of being a despirited body (dry meat) or the terror of being a disembodied Spirit (thin vapor).[47]

Allowing the natural compensating and balancing workings of the Yin/Yang Ch'i dynamics of Heavenly Tao to be operating in the attending relationship/process and are assisting human beings in allowing positive energies to be balancing negative ones without manipulating or imbalancing their compensating and possibly be increasing symptoms, e.g., in iatrogenic/physician-induced illnesses and by using medications whose side-effects are being worse than the conditions that they were prescribed to treat.[48]

Embodying the sufficiency and abundance of Tao and Virtuosity/Te and having seemingly inexhaustible vital energy/Ch'i to be offering for the benefit of human beings in the attending relationship/process without burning-out and to be completing their work without needing gratitude, claiming credit or displaying their excellence.

EXPERIENCE 78

POWER OF GENTLENESS

Nothing in our whole world
Is being more soft and fluid than water
Yet, nothing is surpassing it
For overcoming hard and rigid
Nothing is replacing it

Our whole world is knowing
Fluidity is overcoming rigidity
Softness is overcoming hardness
Yet, few of us are practicing it

As wise human beings, we are saying:
Bearing the inner shame of our State
Is being custodian of the land
Enduring the outer misery of our State
Is being steward of the world

True words are seeming paradoxical

Synopsis 78 ❖ Power of Gentleness

Soft and fluid are overcoming hard and rigid; like flowing water is gentle, yielding and conforming yet is softening, smoothing and dissolving. This is being known by many people, yet few are living what they are knowing. Wise human beings are being custodians and stewards of the Tao-State, the land and the world, the Earth and its beings, by identifying with, bearing and enduring the inner shame of human beings and the outer miseries of the human condition.

Commentary 78 ❖ Power of Gentleness

Wise attenders are:

Among the few professionals who are embodying and utilizing their water-like softness, gentleness and fluidity in effectively working with hard times, rough spots and rigid forces during the attending relationship/process, e.g., defensive resistances, interpersonal con-flicts, transference projections, power struggles, deadlocked impasses and acting-out.

Experiencing that soft, gentle and flexible contacts, connections and interactions with human beings, like the power of persistently flow-ing water, are instrumental in naturally softening, loosening, eroding, smoothing and dissolving their rigid defenses, solid resistances, tight controls, fixed patterns, hardened behaviors and sclerotic routines.

Empathizing with, introjecting and identifying with the shame, guilt, misery and suffering of human beings in the attending relation-ship/process, as well as that of humanity in the world at large and, as such, are custodians, trustees, stewards and caretakers of the Tao-State and the myriad phenomena and vicissitudes of collective human being, existing, experiencing and living.[49]

Experience 79

Full Responsibility

As great grievances are being reconciled
Some discontent is usually remaining
How is this being made good?

As wise human beings:
We are owning our part in the matters
Without blaming the other parties

Being with Virtuosity
We are fulfilling agreements
Being without Virtuosity
We are demanding reciprocations

Heaven's Tao is being impartial
And constantly serving goodness

SYNOPSIS 79 ❖ FULL RESPONSIBILITY

Unreconciled grievances and their residual discontents are being successfully resolved by wise human beings fully accepting their responsibility in matters without blaming the other parties involved. As in contractual financial agreements, they are being concerned with what they are owing to others and not with what is owed to them by others and are responsibly fulfilling their side of agreements rather than vindictively demanding payments from others. Wise human beings are embodying Heaven's Tao by constantly and impartially serving goodness, and the goodness of their Virtuosity/Te is usually eliciting goodness and responsibility in other human beings.

COMMENTARY 79 ❖ FULL RESPONSIBILITY

Wise attenders are:

Reconciling disagreements and resolving grievances in the attending relationship/process by taking full responsibility for the issues and their part in them and not blaming other human beings and, in honoring and fulfilling agreements, are keeping to their part of them and not demanding compliance from other human beings.

Modeling real, true, full and empowering commitment-keeping, responsibility-taking and accountability-owning for human beings; are facilitating their working through the emotional, mental, physical and Spiritual effects of victimization and are supporting their not necessarily wasting precious life-energies seeking restitution and retribution by expecting apologies from, plotting revenge against or exacting punishments upon the heartless and soulless perpetrators of betrayals, violations, abuses, terrors, cruelties, traumas, tortures and horrors.

Embodying and enacting the equality and impartiality of Heavenly Tao by constantly serving the goodness, fairness and kindness of their Virtuosity/Te and that of human beings regardless of positive and negative fluctuations in the attending relationship/process.

EXPERIENCE 80

STATE OF TAO

Here is a small State
With few inhabitants

As human beings:
Though there are one hundred times
The necessary conveniences
We are not using them very much
We are taking dying seriously
And are not traveling very far
Though there are enough vehicles
We are not riding in them
Though there are some weapons
We are not displaying them

As human beings, we are:
Living simply and sufficiently
Being satisfied with our local foods
Being pleased with our plain clothes
Being contented with our small homes
Being delighted with our usual ways

Neighboring communities are within earshot
Of crowing roosters and barking dogs
Yet, as human beings
We are happily growing old and dying
Without going out to visit them

Synopsis 80 ❖ State of Tao

Simplicity, sufficiency and contentment are characterizing the natural primordial State of Tao.[50] Dwelling in/*as* Tao is being satisfied, pleased, fulfilled and delighted in the basics of ordinary and everyday ways of living. Simply being at home in/*as* Tao is allowing human beings to be happily and enjoyably living out their life spans without needing to go out pursuing 'things' or visiting 'others'. The few inhabitants of the small State of Tao are living simply and simply living.

Commentary 80 ❖ State of Tao

Wise attenders are:

Inhabiting the small State of Tao, are few in number with more than the necessary amount of psychotherapy/counseling instruments, techniques and vehicles for working with human beings but are not using or displaying them.

Taking the terminating of the attending relationship/process seriously, are staying within its safe limits and secure boundaries and the phenomenological frame of references of human beings and are not traveling very far away from their Home State of Tao.

Embodying simplicity and sufficiency in the attending relationship/process and are satisfied with the number of human beings with whom they meet, pleased and contented with their abiding contact and residing connection and delighted with the ordinary and everyday conducting of the life of the attending relationship/process just *as* it is.

Being serenely at Home in the State of Tao, are aware of psychotherapists/counselors in the surrounding professional community but are happily living out their attending relationship/processes without going out to network with them.

EXPERIENCE **81**

BENEFITING AND ASSISTING

True words are not always beautiful
Beautiful words are not always true

Developed human beings are not always arguing
Arguing people are not always developed

Wise human beings are not always learned
Learned people are not always wise

As wise human beings:
We are not accumulating
The more we are using for others
The more we are having
The more we are giving to others
The more we are having

Heaven's Tao
Is benefiting, not harming
Wise human beings' Tao
Is assisting, not contending[51]

Synopsis 81 ❖ Benefiting and Assisting

The true words of developed and wise human beings are not being the beautiful words of undeveloped erudite debaters. Wise human beings are generously and charitably giving to and using for human beings and are not accumulating for themselves. Their wealth is proportionate to their donations and contributions. The benefiting and not harming of Heaven's Tao and the assisting and not contending of wise human beings are an identity.

Commentary 81 ❖ Benefiting and Assisting

Wise attenders are:

Truly communicating and conversing (turning together) with human beings in the attending relationship/process openly, clearly, concretely, directly, honestly and wholeheartedly without using beautiful words, debating or disputing issues or delivering intellectualized monologues or erudite discourses.

Not seeking, pursuing, acquiring or accumulating anything in the attending relationship/process, e.g., referrals, theories, techniques, insights, catharses, outcomes, 'cures', validation, status, wealth, etc. and are generously and charitably giving and using who they are being and what they are having to/for human beings out of a wholehearted commitment to their health, welfare, well-being and happiness.

Identifying *as* the constancy and openness of Tao; the potency and efficacy of Virtuosity/Te; the alternating, harmonizing and reversing of Yin/Yang Ch'i dynamics; the flowing, circulating and returning of Wu Wei Ch'i kinetics and the naturalness and spontaneity of Tzu Jan and are engaging human beings in the attending relationship/process as a rare and precious opportunity to be freely exploring, openly discovering, deeply experiencing, fully actualizing and joyfully sharing their absolutely unique reality, truth, goodness, kindness and beauty.

Serving, encouraging, supporting, assisting, facilitating, guiding and not contending with human beings in the attending relationship/process and are being identical with Heavenly Tao and its benefiting of all beings and harming of none.[52]

FAN **CH'ENG**

RETURN/RETURN TO COMPLETE/FINISH
REVERSE/REVERT TO PERFECT/FULFILL
GOING BACK TO RIPEN/MATURE
COMING BACK TO ACCOMPLISH/SUCCEED

A MATURE/DEVELOPED INDIVIDUAL WARRIOR RUNNING/
STOPPING/TURNING AROUND/COMING BACK/RETURNING/
REVERTING TO TAO

THE CONCLUDING/COMPLETING/CONSUMMATING/CULMINATING
EXPERIENCE OF HUMAN BEING/BEING HUMAN IS EMBODYING/
PERSONIFYING/IDENTIFYING *AS* TAO AND ITS CHARACTERISTICS/
ATTRIBUTES/QUALITIES/ACTIVITIES IN THE AWAKENED
CONSCIOUSNESS AND NATURAL LIVING OF SACRED/WISE
HUMAN BEINGS

CONCLUSION

This rendition of Lao Tzu's *Tao Te Ching* and the psychother-apeutic commentaries are being concluded with the application of the principal experiential concepts considered to psychother-apy/counseling and with some material on patients/counselees, psychotherapists/counselors and psychotherapy/counseling.

Application of Concepts

The principal experiential concepts being identified in this rendition are: A constant (Tao), coherently individualizing (Te), consistently energizing (Ch'i), continually transforming (Yin/Yang Ch'i), continuously flowing (Wu Wei Ch'i) and sponta-neously presencing (Tzu Jan) as myriad phenomena (Wan Wu) completed in the awakened consciousnesses of Tao-embodied, Tao-personified and Tao-identified Sacred and wise human beings (Sheng Jen).

Each of the principal experiential concepts is affording a way of deconditioning and re-experiencing the bodies, minds, selves, Souls and Spirits of human beings in the attending relationship/process by:

Tao	re-awakening and realizing the Ultimate Reality of Tao *as* our transcendent context/origin/agency.
Te	re-instating and re-establishing the Virtuosity/potency/efficacy of our uniquely individual innate/inner Tao-nature.
Ch'i	re-viving and replenishing the pervading/animating/activating/sustaining vitality of our primordial energy.

Yin/Yang Ch'i	re-polarizing and re-pairing the separate/opposed/mutually exclusive dualities in our conscious experiencing into bipolar/alternating/centering/voiding/reversing complements.
Wu Wei Ch'i	re-sourcing and re-activating the frictionlesss/effortless/seamless/flowing/circulating/unfolding/cycling/completing/returning of our ongoing activities.
Sheng Jen	recovering and reowning our Sacredness, dignity, wisdom and humanity.
Tzu Jan	renewing and refreshing the naturalness/spontaneity/presencing of our ongoing experiencing.
Wan Wu	reframing and revisioning the myriad/diverse/rich phenomenal actualities of our subjective experiencing *as* immanent Tao.

Table One

The following table is illustrating how the principal experiential concepts considered in this rendition can be applied to organize some common constituents and characteristics of the attending relationship/process.

Tao	*Te*	*Ch'i*	*Yin/Yang Ch'i*
Context	Uniqueness	Energy	Changes
Principle	Potency	Pathways	Polarity
Paradigm	Potentiality	Patterns	Parity
Reality	Individuality	Vitality	Complementarity
Ultimacy	Integrity	Agency	Alternating
Constancy	Authenticity	Regulating	Counterbalancing
Unity	Efficacy	Economy	Centralizing
Identity	Virtuosity	Efficiency	Reversing

Wu Wei Ch'i	*Tzu Jan*	*Wan Wu*	*Sheng Jen*
Interventions	Naturalness	Content	Human Beings
Process	Presencing	Phenomena	Participating
Proceeding	Playing	Panorama	Partnership
Flowing	Originality	Phenomenality	Humanness
Yielding	Creativity	Multiplicity	Wisdom
Following	Spontaneity	Variety	Humility
Unfolding	Serendipity	Diversity	Intimacy
Returning	Freedom	Totality	Sacredness

Table Two

The following table is using four of the principal experiential concepts in this rendition and their modalities to illustrate some characteristic psychotherapy/counseling focuses and activities of traditional and/or alternative, complementary and integrative approaches.

CONCEPT
  Te

MODALITY
  Knowing/Noetic

TRADITIONAL
  Behavioral interpreting
  Conceptual analyzing
  Theoretical formulating
  Diagnostic assessing

COMPLEMENTARY
  Presuppositionless/
  preconceptual
  awareness/witnessing/
  describing
  of phenomena[53]
  Attending/accepting
  Respecting/receiving

CONCEPT
  Yin/Yang Ch'i

MODALITY
  Having/Dynamic

TRADITIONAL
  Coping skills assessing
  Ego-strength evaluating
  Clinical judging
  Case formulating

COMPLEMENTARY
  Considering/
  reflecting upon the
  alternating/bipolarity/
  reversing
  of experiencing
  Attuning/according
  Reflecting/reciprocating

CONCEPT
  Wu Wei Ch'i

MODALITY
  Doing/Kinetic

TRADITIONAL
  Goal setting
  Treatment planning
  Intervention strategizing
  Methods/techniques

COMPLEMENTARY
  Yielding/following
  the flowing/unfolding/
  returning of process
  Allowing/accompanying
  Re-Sourcing/responding

CONCEPT
  Tao

MODALITY
  Being/Ontic

TRADITIONAL
  Prognostic speculating
  End-setting
  Termination determining
  Outcome evaluating

COMPLEMENTARY
  Intersubjective/collaborative
  frame of reference
  for completing treatment
  Affiliating/allying
  Reconnecting/reuniting

Patients/Counselees

So-called 'patients/counselees' are being referred to throughout this rendition as human beings who are engaging in the attending relationship/process. Typically, they are seeking assistance in their lives by entering into psychotherapy/counseling because they are, for whatever reason, unable to find, access or utilize relevant, appropriate and effective resources within themselves or among other human beings in their lives. As such, they often are relatively isolated, needful and vulnerable.

Most human beings voluntarily coming to, entering into and engaging in psychotherapy/counseling are typically presenting with some of the following clustering of concerns . . .

Abilities to actualize	Issues to settle
Addictions to remit	Living to improve
Anger to control	Objectives to accomplish
Anxiety to reduce	Obsessions to stop
Behaviors to change	Pain to alleviate
Blocks to release	Plans to implement
Challenges to meet	Potentials to realize
Compulsions to eliminate	Problems to solve
Conflicts to resolve	Questions to answer
Confusions to understand	Relationships to repair
Depression to lift	Shame to abate
Difficulties to overcome	Skills to develop
Dignity to regain	Stress to manage
Energy to have	Successes to achieve
Esteem to raise	Suffering to end
Fears to conquer	Symptoms to ameliorate
Guilt to cease	Tasks to complete
Habits to break	Tensions to relieve
Hopes to realize	Worries to dispel
Impulses to regulate	Worth to recover
Inhibitions to express	Wounds to heal

. . . as well as those of psychotic delusions and hallucinations, personality and behavior disorders, post-traumatic flashbacks and nightmares, bi-polar alternatings and cyclings, suicidal ideation and impulses, physical disabilities and/or terminal illnesses and a host of other concerns and conditions to cope, deal and work with and to change, transform, eliminate or accept in order to get on with living a reasonably functional, successful, meaningful, satisfying, fulfilling and/or enjoyable life.

Regardless of particular issues, needs, motives and abilities; most human beings engaging in psychotherapy/counseling are appreciative of and encouraged, supported, assisted and benefited by being openly received, warmly contacted, fully listened to; regarded with respect, interest and enthusiasm; and related to with impartiality, equality and empathy.

As such, human beings are usually feeling safe, secure and trusting enough to be communicated and connected with; to begin to feel rapport, relax defenses and soften resistances; to establish a cooperative and collaborative working therapeutic alliance; and to embark upon their unique journey of self-exploration, discovery, understanding, regulating, healing, transforming, developing, actualizing, etc..

Human beings engaging in the attending relationship/process are being regarded and held by wise attenders with validity and legitimacy, value and worth and honor and dignity as absolutely unique, whole and capable individuals whose inner Tao-nature, Virtuosity/Te and the efficacious power of their innate gifts, inborn talents and inherent genius are their inner resources for efficiently and effectively reconstituting their experiencing of themselves and their Beings, Lives, Selves, Souls and Spirits.

Psychotherapists/Counselors

So-named 'psychotherapists/counselors' are being referred to throughout this rendition as wise attenders. They are human beings who are personally and professionally called to, committed to and engaged in conducting a psychotherapy/counseling practice. Wise attenders are Tao-focused, Tao-centered and Tao-identified and are embodying, personifying and enacting some of the characteristics, qualities, traits and activities of the experiential concepts described in this rendition and its commentaries as follows:

Being Te-Like
Inner Tao-nature
Uniqueness/individuality
Potency/efficacy
Integrity/Virtuosity
Letting-be
Awake/accepting
Respecting/receiving
Not externalizing
Not objectifying
Not abstracting
Clear-minded
Sanity/sagacity

Being Yin/Yang Ch'i-Like
Bipolarity/interdependence
Complementarity/mutuality
Equality/reciprocity
Balancing/centering
Letting-go
Attuning/according
Reflecting/relinquishing
Not attaching
Not evaluating
Not judging
Empty-hearted
Simplicity/sufficiency

Being Wu Wei Ch'i-Like
Flexible/flowing
Frictionless/effortless
Yielding/following
Conforming/cooperating
Going-with
Allowing/accompanying
Re-Sourcing/responding
Not controlling

Being Tao-Like
Transcendent/immanent
Nondual/integral
Unity/identity
Whole/complete
Being-with
Affiliating/abiding
Reuniting/residing
Not distancing

Not forcing
Not contending
Still-willed
Serenity/synergy

Not separating
Not alienating
Pure-Spirited
Safety/security

Being Ch'i-Like

Pervading/nourishing
Conserving/economizing
Cultivating/compounding
Efficient/effective
Being-alive
Animating/activating
Revitalizing/rejuvenating
Not depleting
Not draining
Not wasting
Fully-energized
Supporting/sustaining

Being Tzu Jan-Like

Natural/spontaneous
Self-so/Self-like
Present/immediate
Creative/innovative
Being-free
Appearing/appreciating
Recreating/refreshing
Not rehearsing
Not performing
Not replaying
Freely-presencing
Spontaneity/serendipity

Being Wan Wu-Like

Materiality/physicality
Phenomenality/experiential
Variety/diversity
Multiplicity/totality
Being-all
Actuality/array
Revealing/realizing
Not 'things'
Not egos
Not 'others'
Objectively formed
Subtlety/splendor

Being Sheng Jen-Like

Sacred/wise
Egoless/universal
Tao-embodied/centered
Tao-personified/identified
Being-human
Available/accessible
Real/respectful
Not claiming
Not displaying
Not priding
Humanly be-ing
Sacredness/Spirituality

Wise attenders are typically being and doing more/less of the following activities in the attending relationship/ process as categorized by four principal experiential concepts and their modalities and states.

Te-Like — Knowing/mental/no 'thing'-knowing/No-thing/ Tao- 'knowing'/letting-be

More/less

Concretizing/abstracting	Witnessing/diagnosing	Specifying/generalizing
Experiencing/analyzing	Receiving/formulating	Paraphrasing/discussing
Reflecting/conceptualizing	Discovering/theorizing	Clarifying/concluding
Describing/interpreting	Listening/speaking	Normalizing/pathologizing
Understanding/explaining	Inquiring/lecturing	Empowering/strengthening

Yin/Yang Ch'i-Like — Having/emotional/no 'thing'-having/ No-thing/Tao-'having'/letting-go

More/less

Appreciating/evaluating	Complementing/opposing	Reversing/transposing
Centralizing/externalizing	Harmonizing/conflicting	Simplifying/attenuating
Polarizing/dualizing	Regulating/controlling	Suggesting/reinforcing
Balancing/weighting	Stabilizing/catalyzing	Encouraging/challenging
Compensating/correcting	Equalizing/preferring	Dialoguing/monologuing

Wu Wei Ch'i-Like — Doing/volitional/no 'thing'-doing/No-thing/ Tao-'doing'/going-with

More/less

Exploring/planning	Conforming/asserting	Developing/constructing
Following/leading	Complying/managing	Unfolding/implementing
Guiding/directing	Yielding/resisting	Evolving/devising
Allowing/intervening	Responding/initiating	Assisting/helping
Acceding/evoking	Pacing/strategizing	Facilitating/augmenting

Tao-Like — Being/relational/no 'thing'-being/No-thing/ Tao-'being'/being-with

More/less

Meeting/interviewing	Connecting/objectifying	Empathizing/confronting
Attending/observing	Joining/separating	Unifying/dividing
Communing/interacting	Allying/cooperating	Returning/repeating
Including/selecting	Disclosing/unrevealing	Integrating/summarizing
Engaging/distancing	Supporting/reinforcing	Completing/terminating

These activities are not exhausting all of the 'mores/lesses' engaged in by wise attenders and are not necessarily equally inclusive bipolar complements or mutually exclusive dualistic opposites.

Wise human beings are utilizing some of the following kernals of wisdom found in the eight principal experiential concepts of this rendition in conducting the attending relationship/process.

Tao/Nondual Reality

Framing psychotherapy/counseling in a larger transpersonal context and relativizing a strictly psychological level of observation and understanding.

Acknowledging Spirit, Mystery, nondual Unity and integral Identity as the psychospiritual Reality of human beings.

Joining the existential/phenomenological/experiential reality of human beings and engaging in the intersubjective/dialogical/integral attending relationship/process just *as* it is.

Te/Unique Virtuosity

Embodying the power of presence and not the presence of power.

Trusting in the goodness and rightness of the unique innate Tao-nature, native intelligence, common sense, inherent wisdom, inner truth and intrinsic genius of human beings.

Empowering human beings without overdeveloping power to accelerate change, growth and transformation.

Yin/Yang Ch'i/Balancing Energy

Conserving and not wasting vital energy and cultivating life force rather than force life.

Experiencing the usefulness of the empty inner centerspace of the plenum void at its maximum to manifest forms.

Using bipolarity, complementarity and equality as a model for intrapsychic experiences and interpersonal relationships and their alternating, balancing, centering and reversing.

Wu Wei Ch'i/Flowing Activity

Being the water-like frictionless, effortless and seamless flowing of the attending relationship/process.

Not controlling, forcing, manipulating, exploiting or otherwise interfering with human beings and their lives.

Complying with, cooperating with and not resisting; and supporting, assisting and facilitating what is going on as it is naturally proceeding, unfolding, developing and completing.

Sheng Jen/Wise Humanity

Being Tao-centered, Tao-identified and Tao-like without ego-projects, personal agendas, self-interests and professionalistic personas, positions and postures.

Cultivating deep and transparent connections with human beings and impartially and empathically identifying with their essential universality and existential individuality as absolutely unique Selves and Human Souls.

Not seeking name, fame, status, reputation, credit, gratitude and gain through psychotherapy/counseling work.

Honoring the calling of a Sacred and wise human being as 'one who listens, hears, understands, obeys and speaks'.

Tzu Jan/Spontaneous Presencing

Being natural, spontaneous, free, Self-like, Self-so and As-Is.

Appreciating the constant, continual and continuous presencing of all human beings and experiences just as they are, of themselves so.

Enjoying the creative 'playing' of Tao in the universe of human existence and the world of human experience.

Wan Wu/Phenomenal Actuality

Experiencing the phenomenal (in both senses of the word) actuality and totality of the myriad variety and diversity of human beings, experiences, objects, activities and events as holographic microcosms of immanent Tao.

Experiencing the culminating panoramic Mysteries of origination, Miracles of formation, Marvels of manifestation and Magnificence of completion of everything.

Treasuring the precious art (Virtuosity) of the State (Tao) and also the ordinary state (present condition) of the art (craft of psychotherapy/counseling).

Attributing causality, agency, potency and efficacy to a Superordinate Reality, e.g., Tao, or to a Higher Power, e.g., God; does not involve abdicating professional responsibility for the nature, characteristics, effects, results, outcomes and consequences of activities and actions in the attending relationship/process. Rather, authentic personal accountability exists to a deeper degree, at a higher level and to a fuller extent when true attenders are free of ego-needs, investments and attachments and are truthfully and humbly identified as intuitve mediums, channels and conduits for; and embodied instruments, vehicles and conveyances of, the Spiritual context, reality and energies of the attending relationship/process, regardless of the particular nature, focus and forms of the psychotherapeutic work.

Psychotherapy/Counseling

Psychotherapy/counseling as a social institution, human resource and professional service may be becoming an endangered species due to our ignorance and arrogance and one that is requiring significant attention to protect, sustain and propogate it.

Historically, the field of psychotherapy/counseling succeeded partially because it was part of a larger medical enterprise predicated upon human beings', e.g.,

❖ Ignorance of, and distrust in, the natural workings of the human body, mind and Self.

❖ Intolerance of pain, suffering, conflicts and uncontrollable 'negative' experiences.

❖ Fears of disease, illness, disability, degeneration, deterioration and death.

❖ Unquestioned belief in, and unexamined projections onto, medical authority figures.

❖ Abdicating one's own authentic authorship and authoritativeness of self and life.

❖ Ignorance of the healing and transforming power of human Consciousness and energy.

❖ Systematic excluding of the Human Soul and Spirit from a materialistic, reductionistic and monolithic medical disease model and treatment ethic.

Currently, there appears to be a general decline in human beings' seeking out and utilizing psychotherapy/counseling resources to assist them in their life journeying for a *numb-er* of reasons, e.g.,

❖ The overprescribing and using of psychiatric medications to treat symptoms only.

❖ Insurance companies limiting the kinds of conditions covered and reimbursed for.

❖ Managed health care limiting the number of sessions treatment providers can have.

❖ Private practitioners desiring longer-term patients and requiring higher-fee practices.

❖ The popularity of self-help gurus, weekend workshops, trends, fads and gimmicks.

❖ Ego-identified vicarious 'living' through TV, movies, spectator sports and celebrities.

❖ The proliferation and using of absorbing and distracting technological devices (e-living).

❖ A fast-food, quick-fix and cyber-speed mentality with regard to being and living (e-being).

❖   Web sites, quasi-information, social networking and
     psuedo-relationships on the Internet (e-relating).

There still are many dedicated psychotherapists/counselors
who are committed to preserving and/or restoring the real and
true humanness of one-to-one individual psychotherapy/coun-
seling. Wise ones are experiencing the attending relationship,
essentially, as a synchronistic meeting of two human beings at
the juncture of their uniquely individual life journeys who both
are wayfaring companions having something of mutual benefit
to discover, develop, actualize and share together.

Wise psychotherapy/counseling can be considered as assisting human beings in working through conditions and issues that
are in the way of their Soul-progressing, transforming and transitioning from conditioned psychophysical/psychosocial identifications with body, mind, ego, others and world to awakened
psychospiritual realities of Spirit, Consciousness, Self, Being
and the Multiverse, e.g.,

From	To
Unconscious/asleep/dream	Conscious/awake/aware
Conditioned/collective/masses	Unconditioned/individual/unique
Material/impersonal/contents	Spiritual/transpersonal/context
Closed/bound/limited ego	Open/free/spacious Self
Dualistic/differential/'things'	Nondual/integral/Being
Separate/divided/fragments	United/undivided/wholes
Ego-image/persona/facade	Real/true/genuine/Self
Outer/externally directed	Inner/internally connected
Schism/empty/dark hole	Embodied/body-Spirit
Disembodied Spirit/terror	EnSouled/incorporation/gratitude
Spasm/solid/dark mass	InSpirited/Spirit-body
Despirited body/horror	EnSouled/animation/beatiude
The '10,000 things' of immanent Tao	The Unity of transcendent Tao

The wise psychotherapy/counseling experience is a small,
brief and precious arc sometime and somewhere in the middle,

center and Heart of a Great Life Cycle of birthing, living and dying. Our unique life-long wayfaring from the 10,000 things/ Wan Wu of intimate experiencing to the Oneness of Ultimate Tao, as our inner Tao-nature/Virtuosity/Te, is identical to the journeying of our Human Soul from ego-identifying with body, mind, others and world to *being* the Reality of our Human Spirit, Psyche, Being and Universe.

In addition to working with the presenting issues and concerns of human beings, wise psychotherapy/counseling is a special complementary opportunity to be awakening to ourselves as journeying and wayfaring Souls and to be consciously living a Tao/Spirit-focused, Tao/Spirit-centered, Tao/Spirit-identified and Tao/Spirit-like life as Human Beings; and to be cultivating, developing, experiencing, fulfilling and sharing the innate gift, inborn genius, inherent power and intrinsic goodness of our absolutely and uniquely individualized Virtuosity/ Te, our inner Tao-nature and Human Soul. Including Spirit and our Human Soul into the mix, co-creates psychotherapy/ counseling as Consciousness-awakening, Self-transforming and Life-changing.[54/55]

Wise psychotherapy/counseling is taking place in our Homeland and Heartland, the pristine, uncharted wilderness and open space wherein our Mind's truth and wisdom are Tao's Light, our Heart's beauty and harmony are Tao's Love, our Will's grace and peace are Tao's Law and our Being's reality and joy are Tao's Life and which is a deep and quiet place like no other one and where no one has ever gone and been before. . . . . .

NOTES

1. The meaning of all of the Chinese language characters depicted in this rendition are based upon etymological definitions of their radicals and phonetics and philosophical extensions in their usage.

2. In this rendition, some qualities of Tao are Tao as:
    1. Hidden - Mystery
    2. Formed - Miracles
    3. Manifested - Marvels
    4. Completed - Magnificence
    5. Celestial spaciousness - Heaven
    6. Terrestrial groundedness - Earth
    7. Existential centeredness - Human Being
    8. Primordial Simplicity - Unhewn wood/P'u
                              - Unspun silk/Ssu

3. Ch'i is the all-pervading/animating vital energy constituting/condensing as/circulating within and sustaining/regulating/harmonizing/stabilizing everything in the cosmic universe and the human body. Ch'i is both primordial and acquired and has the following characteristics:

PRIMORDIAL CH'I	ACQUIRED CH'I
Prenatal/endowed	Postnatal/derived
Inner Breath	Outer breath
Heavenly/spacious	Earthly/grounded
Nonmaterial/rarefied	Material/condensed
Ubiquitous/universal	Spatio-temporal/individualized
Undifferentiated/constant	Differentiated/changing
Inexhaustible	Exhaustible
Needs to be gathered/ preserved	Needs to be cultivated/ conserved
Transcendent Tao	Immanent Tao

Ch'i is identical to Tao. Yin/Yang Ch'i is alternating, counterbalancing and reversing Ch'i and Wu Wei Ch'i is flowing, circulating and returning Ch'i. Heavenly/cosmic Ch'i is spacious, Earthly/worldly Ch'i is grounded and Human/embodied Ch'i is centered in the Heart.

4. Te is most often translated as 'virtue' and/or 'power'. In this rendition, it is being understood as 'Virtuosity', according to its English dictionary definition of 'Great technical skill in the practice of a fine art'. Qualities of Te are: inner Tao-nature, innate wisdom, inborn genius, inherent potency, intrinsic efficacy and individual integrity. Te is perfect and complete compliance and harmony with the natural laws of the universe and the essential requirements of situations and is the ability to perfectly embody and enact the reality, truth, goodness and rightness of one's unique being, gifts, capacities and potentials.

5. Yin/Yang occurs only once in Passage 42 of the *Tao Te Ching* where Yin is 'carried on the back' and Yang is 'embraced in the front'. There are, however, over one-hundred twenty-five dynamically interrelated bipolar complements referred to throughout the text.

Yin/Yang Ch'i interrelationships, interchangings and interactions originate all of the phenomena in the universe and their activities, changes, transformations and reversals.

Primordial Ch'i differentiates into Yin Ch'i and Yang Ch'i which are integrated with the Nonultimate immaterial primal void of Nonbeing/Wu Chi as T'ai Chi, the Supreme Ultimate which further differentiates into Heaven, Earth and Human Being, the twin Spiritual Soul/Hun and physical Soul/P'o of human beings and the '10,000 things'/Wan Wu of existence and experience.

All phenomena of Nature (Heaven-Earth), life and human existence and experience manifest the dynamic interrelationships of Yin/Yang Ch'i bipolar energies in a complementary, interdependent and mutually inclusive both-and way. One-sided, either-or, mutually exlusive and fixed dualities are contrary to the natural alternating, counterbalancing, centering, voiding and reversing of Yin/Yang Ch'i dynamics and characterize most all of the oppositions, antagonisms and conflicts in human existence, relationships and experience.

6. Wu Wei Ch'i activities are those of no 'thing'-doing and Tao-sourced actions that conform to and comply with the natural laws, organic rhythms and ongoing processes of Nature, Heaven-Earth, life, world and human existing and experiencing. They are essential and necessary actions that are appropriate, fitting and suitable for given circumstances rather than those planned, implemented and executed to effect, achieve and accomplish particular purposes, aims, goals, objectives, results and outcomes. Wu Wei Ch'i actions are responsive and yield to, allow and follow the natural frictionless, effortless and seamless proceeding and unfolding of events without interfering with or attempting to control, force or manipulate them.

7. Yin/Yang Ch'i is governed by the Law of Reversal, such that when one pole of a given bipolarity reaches its maximum, it naturally reverts to its counterpart, e.g., in systolic/contracting and diastolic/expanding cardiac rhythms and the inspiration/expanding and expiration/contracting respiratory cycle. Wu Wei Ch'i is governed by the Law of Return, such that the unfolding of flowing processes naturally return to their origin, e.g., in the arterial outflowing and venous inflowing coursing of the circulatory system and in the cycling of the seasons and the life cycle. An illustrative analogy is that of the mechanism and movements of a non-digital clock where 'tic-toc' is the rhythmical alternating and reversing of Yin/Yang Ch'i and the dial hands are the cyclical rotating and returning of Wu Wei Ch'i.

When, for example, pain and depression are fully experienced, they become an experience of fullness rather than just pain and depression, by reaching a maximum and then reverting and returning to the original emptiness of experiencing. But it is difficult for most of us to allow and to go deeper and further into many intense 'negative' experiences and to let them maximize and fully complete themselves rather than abate or abort them in some way, e.g., by using pain killing or mood elevating medications. However, often when some symptoms are left to run their course, they do naturally revert and return to being asymptomatic, e.g., fevers break, antibodies go to work and healing crises pass.

8. Tzu Jan is the self-so/self-like nature of phenomena that are spontaneously presencing of-themselves-so and just *as* they are, just-so, *as*-such, *as*-is in the sheerly and utterly perfect givenness of human experiencing. They are the happenings and serendipitous occurrences that are unconditioned, unintended, unconstrued, unplanned, unrehearsed, unrepeated etc. and which are alive, novel, fresh, immediate and surprising. They are just what *is* prior to making some 'thing' out of them by separating, externalizing, objectifying, abstracting, defining, naming, evaluating, judging, preferring, attaching, investing, interfering, etc.. And Wan Wu are those myriad, varied and diverse phenomena, beings, things, contents, forms and activities, etc. of human being, existence and living that are appearing in consciousness and awareness as immanent microcosmic/holographic manifestations and correspondences of transcendent macrocosmic Tao.

9. Sheng Jen are Sacred and wise human beings referred to as sages. They are embodying, internalizing, assimilating, enacting, personifying and identifying *as* Tao and their Tao-nature. They are living Tao-focused, Tao-centered, Tao-returned and Tao-like lives and are being the characteristics, qualities and activities of Virtuosity/Te, Yin/Yang Ch'i dynamics, Wu Wei Ch'i kinetics and Tzu Jan spontaneous presencing.

Sheng Jen have made the transformation from an ego-'thing'/Wo Wu to a Tao-Self/Tao Tzu; have found Reality in the illusions of 'ego', Truth in the fictions of 'others', Light in the mirages of 'world' and Beauty in the deadness of 'things' and are the conclusion, completion, consummation and culmination of Tao. Sheng Jen are free of ignorance, attachment, error and separation by being mentally clear, emotionally empty, volitionally still and relationally one. They are receiving like a deep valley, reflecting like a clear mirror, responding like a quick echo and refreshing like pure water. Sheng Jen embrace all beings impartially and equally, are one with all activities and events and are intimately involved and uniquely participating in the universe, cosmic and world process.

Sheng Jen are upholding, backing and siding with fellow human beings by humbly relating below, behind and beside them and are supporting, nourishing, assisting, facilitating, guiding and benefiting them. They naturally exert a unifying, transforming, harmonizing and developing in-fluence (inflowing) upon human beings and their surroundings by their presence alone.

Sheng Jen are the Heart and Soul of Tao, the Bosom of Spirit, the Beacon of Light, the Gift of Life and the Chalice of Love. Their kindness, goodness, gentleness and friendliness are the Truth, Beauty, Grace and Reality that bring wisdom, harmony, peace and joy to human beings and human living. As such, Sheng Jen are the world's greatest and most precious treasure.

A comparison of Sheng Jen, the Sacred/wise human beings of Lao Tzu's *Tao Te Ching*, and Chen Jen, the true/free human beings of Chuang Tzu's *Nei P'ien*, is made in the Prologue of the companion rendition, *Chuang Tzu's Nei P'ien: Psychotherapeutic Commentaries. A Wayfaring Counselor's Rendering of the Seven Interior Records.*

10. An electricity analogy is useful in explicating these eight principal experiential concepts as follows:

Tao — The pre-existing no-'thing'-ness of pure potential.

Yin/Yang Ch'i — The positive-negative potential difference creating an electrical charge.

Ch'i — The power/force of electrical energy.

Wu Wei Ch'i — The flowing electrical energy in the circuit.

Te - the on/off switch and/or rheostat for activating the flash-point and/or regulating the intensity of the electrical current.

Tzu Jan — The spontaneous presencing of the visible effects of the electrical current, e.g., light/heat.

Wan Wu — The materially resistant things activated by the electrical current, e.g., a lightbulb filament or heating element.

Sheng Jen — The wise human beings operating the switch/rheostat, utilizing and, hopefully, conserving the electrical energy.

11.   The eight principal experiential concepts can be applied to psychotherapy/counseling as ways of, and models for, considering:
Psychotherapeutic principle/paradigm (Tao).
Psychotherapeutic power/potentiality (Te).
Psychotherapeutic pathways/patterns (Ch'i).
Psychotherapeutic polarity/parity (Yin/Yang)
Psychotherapeutic process/practice (Wu Wei).
Psychotherapeutic presencing/'playing' (Tzu Jan).
Psychotherapeutic phenomena/panorama (Wan Wu).
Psychotherapeutic partnership/participation (Sheng Jen).

12.   During the microlab basic counseling skills training of psychology graduate students, fully attending and clearly listening were found to create experiences of safe contact and deep connection that opened the way to rapport; self-disclosure, genuine communication, self-awareness, insight and expresson without the necessity of utilizing other facilitative skills.

13.   The Chinese character 'Fei' is defined as no-/not-/not-so/not-like/opposite of/contrary to/apart from/over against/wrong/mistake/false; hence, most all translations read something like 'The Tao that can be expressed is *not* the Constant Tao'. But if Tao is everything, how can there be anything that is 'not-Tao'? The character is a primitive showing two sides opposite of, but back to back and near to, each other and is rendered 'counterpart' in Passage 1 and 'not cultivating Tao' in Passage 53.

14. The lines of this passage are typically translated something like 'Without desires/Wu Yu, perceive the inner subtle Mystery/Hsuan and with desires/Yu, perceive the outer manifest forms/Chiao'. In this rendition, 'thought' is used instead of 'desires' so as to include both desire-based mental/cognitive/thinking and emotional/affective/feeling activities.

Chiao is usually defined and translated as boundary/border/limit/outer form/external manifestation/end. In this rendition, 'Chiao' is 1) considered in the sense of having an 'edge' and the formation of an edge, not as an interface or shared boundary, but as an outer limit/margin that ends in open space and is 2) regarded as a Miracle. The space between the edges, e.g., of our bodies, mediates our separateness, regulates our optimal relatedness and enables intimate edge to edge contact, connection and exquisitely 'edgeless' merging.

Some characteristics of thought-free glimpsing of eternal Mystery and thought-full beholding of infinite Miracles are the following ones:

Thought-Free	Thought-Full
Consciousness without objects	Consciousness of objects
Undifferentiated awareness	Differentiated awareness
Nondual/undivided state	Dualistic/subject-object state
Non-/transphenomenal	Phenomenal
Formless/no-'things'	Forms/things
Field/ground/context	Focus/figure/content
Non-/pre-conceptual reality	Concept-formation
Concept/desire/ego-free	Concept/desire/ego-bound
Witness consciousness	Observing ego
Meditative/contemplative	Cognitive/discursive
Vast/spacious/open	Narrow/limited/closed
Awakened state	Ordinary state

15. Some other examples of this 'identity consciousness' are:
Atman is Brahman   Earth is Heaven
Samsara is Nirvana   The Ordinary is Extraordinary

Karma is Dharma	The '10,000 things' are Tao
Form is Emptiness	Everyday mind is Satori
Shunyata is Tathata	This is It!

16. In the human analogy of conceiving, gestating, birthing and maturing, the Chinese character for gateway/Men signifies the birth canal of the mother/Mu as well as the opening into awakened consciousness and illuminated awareness that all manifesting phenomena are essentially the One Ultimate Spiritual Reality of Tao that identity consciousness is bringing about and being.

17. Most all transformative developmental processes go through four interrelated stages of:

1) The Mystery of origination - creating something from No-'thing'.
2) The Miracle of formation - inner materializing of physical boundaries, limits and edges.
3) The Marvel of manifestation - outer appearing of uniquely individualized being.
4) The Magnificence of completion - culminating of growing, transforming and maturing.

   Prime examples are:
1) Seed planting/germinating/blossoming/foliation and/or fruition.
2) Larval caterpillar/cocoon, pupa, chrysalis/emerging/imago or winged butterfly.
3) Fertile egg/incubating/hatching/fully grown chicken.
4) Human conception/gestation, pregnancy/parturition, birthing/mature human being.
5) Lead or base material/alchemical transmuting/refined material form or gold.
6) Initiating therapy/inner transforming/outer manifesting/terminating.

18. The Mystery of the origination of something from No-thing-ness and the Miracle of the forming of an edge that adjoins only open space are an identity that is the gateway of the Marvels of the manifesting of everything and the Magnificence of their completing.

19. The developing of interdependence, while not necessarily linear, can be understood as the culmination of a progression in human relationships from initially being dependent and co-dependent; to being counter-dependent, independent and non-dependent and finally to being interdependent.

20. Ego is an image and concept of oneself construed through the socially conditioned collective illusions of consensus reality transmitted and modeled by the egos of other human beings. Ego has no real, true or substantial being, is only an illusionary and fictitious imagining and needs to be guarded and defended against being injured or lost. As such, it is fragile and easily dissolved, i.e., it is water soluble; like salt, sugar and fat and, in Spiritual transforming completely disappears in the aqueous medium of the inSpirited human body, being and Tao-nature. Ego is also displaced by the unconditioned Tao-Self, since it cannot co-exist with it at the same higher vibrational frequencies of Spiritual energies and, simply, melts down, drops out, falls away and disappears.

21. A beautiful concretion of, and meditation on, the co-existing of form and emptiness is that of a spherical stone geode. When a geode is being opened, we are observing that the rough outer surface is surrounding and covering an empty inner cavity or centerspace which is lined with a middle layer of clear radiant crystals pointing inward toward its empty and open center.

22. See Note 20. The 'trouble' is not that we have an ego. The ego, fictional entity that it is, serves a useful function in the structuring, organizing, modulating and stabilizing of the psyche as a

whole and the mind-body integrity. Ego-strength and ego-functioning serve as a kind of step-down transformer of, and mediating buffer for, the powerful transformative energies of Spirit. Our mind needs a psychical ego in much the same way that our Spirit has a physical body and the capacity for Spiritual energetic transformation is directly proportionate to the strength of both body and ego. The 'trouble' with the ego is that we can be totally identified with it as who we are as selves and thus eclipse and/or displace our Human Being, Self, Soul and Spirit, e.g., identifying *with* our reflected image in a mirror and not *as* the embodied Spirit/Soul who is looking into it.

23. Benevolence/doing good/Jen, righteousness/being right/I, and propriety/being proper/Li are values, virtues and conduct most often associated with the ethical principles and moral codes being prescribed in Confucianism for instituting, cultivating, governing and maintaining the social order of collective humanity. This way is typically contrasted with characteristics, qualities and activities most often associated with the natural goodness and spontaneous fittingness ascribed in Taoism for self-originating, nourishing, regulating and sustaining the personal harmony of individual human beings, i.e., our inborn Tao-nature and innate Virtuosity/Te.

24. The journey of Self-individuating from the social conditioning and conventional realities of collective humanity is the central focus and process of Analytical/Archetypal Psychology.

25. The Chinese character 'Pu' is usually considered to be a negative/no-/non-/not-/-un and most translations of this Passage read 'not Tao' or 'not Tao-like' for the two lines before the last line. But, again, since everything is Tao, there cannot be anything that is 'not Tao'. The character 'Pu' depicts a bird rising toward, but not reaching, the sky. In this rendition, overdeveloping power is accelerating decay by manipulating Yin/Yang Ch'i dynamics and Wu Wei Ch'i kinetics and these two lines are

rendered as, 'This is not according with Tao' and 'Whatever is not following Tao' in Passages 30 and 55.

26. The essential realities of Yin/Yang Ch'i interactive energy dynamics as female-male can be illustrated by considering human reproductive activity. The male nature of Yang Ch'i is sperm-like, as in the process of conception and reproduction. The male is acting, producing and emitting many sperms in competetive activity to be penetrating and fertilizing the female ovum and to be initiating conception and pregnancy. The female nature of Yin Ch'i is egg-like, as in the process of conception and repro-duction. The female is waiting, receiving and accepting only one sperm in selective activity to be entered and inseminated by the male sperm and to be developing gestation and pregnancy and completing the birthing process.

Male	Female
Many sperms	One egg
Active/moving	Receptive/still
Initiating	Responding
Penetrating/entering	Yielding/opening
Impregnating/conceiving	Gestating/birthing
Outside to inside	Inside to outside

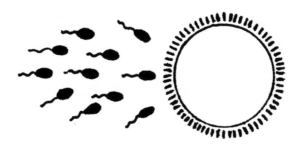

27. Tao is originating and generating, forming and harmoniz-ing and manifesting and completing the cosmogonic sequenc-ing as follows:

0/Wu	1/I	2/Erh	3/San	10,000/Wan
Wu Chi	Yuan Ch'i	Yin/Yang Ch'i	T'ai Chi	Wan Wu
Nonentity	Unity	Bipolarity	Trinity	Totality
Great Void	Great Monad	Great Dyad	Great Triad	Great Myriad
Non-Ultimate	Primordial Energy	Primal Polarity	Supreme Ultimate	10,000 Things

Originating	Generating	Forming	Harmonizing	Manifesting
Sourcing	Producing	Edging	Balancing	Presencing
Mystery	Miracles	Marvels	Magnificence	

Returning to Tao from the '10,000 things' is reversing the cosmogonic sequencing.

28. These and numerous other correspondences are constituting 5 element/agent/Wu Hsing theory.

29. See Note 43 re: uncondition*ed* rather than uncondition*al* love.

30. The diagram below is depicting the sympathetic vibrating and harmonic resonating occurring between wise attenders and human beings during the attending relationship/process over time:

Human Being — unstable/variable/inconsistent/attuning/according frequency

Wise Attender — stable/constant/consistent/maintaining/sustaining frequency

31. The way of this process is most evident in Non-Directive Client/Person-Centered Therapy.

32. See Note 13 re: 'Fei'. Here, again, Fei is not translated as 'not-Tao' but rendered as 'not cultivating Tao'.

33. If something is 'in the way' (obstructing) or 'out of the way' (deviating), it still is the 'Way'.

34. Homage to all of the infants who fell off of their parents' 'big bed' and turned out okay.

35. See Note 25 re: 'Pu'.

36. For example, using grow lights, growth hormones and force feeding to produce and market fruit, vegetables and animals more rapidly. When fruit is picked too early and shipped too far, it is tasteless and quickly passing from green to rotten because of not ripening naturally and being consumed locally.

37. In working with myself and others, I have successfully made a spinal adjustment, freed up an arthritic finger joint, released muscle spasms, healed an ulcer, opened an adhesed Fallopian tube, passed kidney stones, relieved headaches and lowered blood pressure through visualizations, hand passes, energy transmission and discovering the 'message' and meaning in the conditions.

38. The Chinese character 'Kuei' refers to disincarnate, dark and evil spirits; ghosts, goblins, demons and spirits of the dead. 'Phantom' is being used in this rendition to refer to the presence of imaginary beings, psychic entities, fantasy figures, dream images, fictitious apparitions, fictional characters, etc. occurring as phenomena of/in consciousness as well as for insubstantial, disincarnate or disembodied spirits or any other phenomena that are evoking awe, wonder, fear or dread, including symbolic introjects, e.g., residual skeletons in family of origin closets or lingering ghosts of deceased relatives or unresolved relationships.

39. A useful analogy is that of a tightrope walker or high-wire acrobat who is continually making minor compensations and corrections in order to maintain steady balance while moving forward. The earlier that any imbalancing is sensed, the sooner adjustments can be made. When subtle imbalances are sensed, minor shifts can be made more quickly, easily, smoothly and effectively. Early balancing is a subtle vibration and not becoming a larger swaying or rocking movement.

40. The Chinese characters 'Ssu' and 'P'u' are used to signify Primordial Simplicity and, respectively, mean unspun or undyed silk and unhewn or uncarved wood, i.e., natural, raw, original and virginal prior to being 'worked' by human beings. They are referring to our original and undifferentiated Tao-nature.

41. The phenomenological/interpersonal 'space' and the direction and magnitude of the vector of the being of wise human beings and other human beings are:

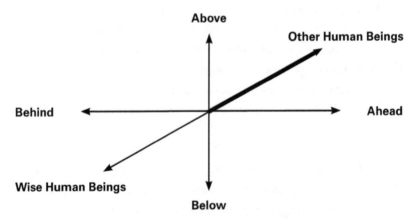

42. In this rendition, the usual order of the '3 Treasures'/San Po of Tao is changed to reflect reserving the vitality of Ching, conserving the energy of Ch'i and preserving the Spirituality of Shen in order to, respectively, be generous, courageous and splendrous.

The following is identifying the 3 Treasures of Tao psychophysically, psychologically and psychospiritually:

Ching	Ch'i	Shen
Semen/Essence	Breath/Vapor	Sacred/Divine
Generative Vitality	Vital Energy	Essential Spirit
Originating of Life	Sustaining of Life	Culminating of Life
Frugality	Compassion	Humility
Economy/Moderation	Deep/Parental Love	Modesty/Deference

Lower Tan T'ien	Middle Tan T'ien	Upper Tan T'ien
Belly Center	Heart Center	Head Center
Reserving Ching	Conserving Ch'i	Preserving Shen
Gathering	Cultivating	Protecting
Accumulating	Compounding	Nourishing
Storing	Circulating	Refining
Reserved Resources	Unconditioned Love	Restrained Precedence
Generous	Courageous	Splendrous

The transformations from vitality to energy to Spirit are usually being undertaken and completed by Chinese Taoist yogic/alchemical adepts/practitioners who are cultivating, transmuting, refining, compounding and circulating energies in the three Tan T'ien/elixir fields and the microcosmic/macrocosmic orbits of the human body. There are numerous alchemical/yogic treatises on this process in the *Taoist Canon/Tao Tsang* and other esoteric Taoist texts.

43. Unconditioned love is being used instead of unconditional love/deep love/parental love/compassion/mercy, as found in most *Tao Te Ching* translations, for several reasons:

1. Unconditional love is an unrealistic ideal and standard of perfection that is impossible to attain due to the conditionality, 'existential facticity' and boundary situations of our being, i.e., the limitations of being a physical body, existing in a social world and living a mortal life.

2. Uncondition*al* love is based upon collectively and socially conditioned learning, understanding, expectations and anticipations about what love and loving relationships are assumed or supposed to be about and set loving human beings up for interpersonal failure and negative self-judgments.

3. Uncondition*ed* loving is accepting the conditionality of living; respecting the limits, boundaries and 'edges' of other human beings; awakening from the ego-trances, fantasies and dreams about what loving is; stopping settling for quid pro quo relationship 'arrangements' and freely, enthusiastically and appreciatively co-creating intimately shared states and qualities of real/true human interbeing.

4. Uncondition*ed* loving is natural and instinctual, personal and transpersonal and Soulful and Spiritual; relatively free of reservations, qualifications, restrictions and requirements; and free of need-based, fantasy-ridden, ideal-bound, compensation-derived, fear-driven, behavior-dependent and deception-laden interpersonal relating.

44. Most translations are reading something like 'There is no greater misfortune than underestimating enemies and losing one's treasures'. In this rendition, it is being proposed that losing the 3 Treasures of Tao is involving conceptually creating and having an 'enemy' in the first place. This is not to deny that, if and when we are encountering someone who is regarding us as their enemy or themselves as our enemy, we should be ignoring, disregarding, underestimating or attempting to rationalize or redefine this reality.

45. See Note 21.

46. Gestalt Therapy avoids intellectualized 'whys' and

abstracted 'aboutisms' and has been succinctly characterized as focusing on the actualities of 'The what and how of the I and Thou in the here and now'.

47. Human beings are being regarded as having twin Souls; the physical/P'o and the Spiritual/Hun Souls which simultaneously are an Earthly embodied Spirit and a Heavenly inspirited body, a body-Spirit and a Spirit-body. Soul-being is the harmonious integrating and radiant identifying of the two which are cultivated and developed through refining body as Spirit and nourishing Spirit as body, i.e., through the inner alchemical/yogic transformings of Ching/Ch'i/Shen and the creating of an immortal fetus, cinnabar pill, blue pearl, philosopher's stone, golden flower, elixir of life, etc.. Otherwise, upon dying, the physical/P'o Soul is descending and returning to Earth and the Spiritual/Hun Soul is ascending and returning to Heaven.

48. TV commercials, in particular, are reporting long lists of side-effects of medications which are as, if not more, troublesome, debilitating, incapacitating, dangerous and lethal than the symptoms and conditions for which they were originally being prescribed to treat. Ridiculously and tragically ironic is the closing caveat to 'Ask your physician if this medication is right for you'.

49. Shamanic healers and exorcists, in particular, are often taking on the illnesses and conditions they are curing and taking in the spirits and entities they are expelling.

50. Other words that are elucidating this Tao-State and quality of Being are: as-is, just-is, as-it-is, just-so, as-such, what-is, what-is-so, of-itself-so, of-its-own-accord, on-its-own, self-like and, as preferred in this rendition, as-itself-so, i.e., Tzu Jan, the natural and spontaneous self-presencing and self-so-ness of Tao, All That Is/As It Is.

51. Usual translations of 'Wei', including the one in this

rendition, relate to 'doing' and 'acting'. However, additional definitions of the character are: be/become/make/cause/practice/act as/serve as/protect/support/help/assist. The latter definition is used in this final passage.

52.   One can come away from a cursory reading of Lao Tzu's *Tao Te Ching* with a superficial impression that the 81 passages are randomly arranged, follow no particular thematic order or are out of coherent order and are, at times, redundant. However, this is typically characteristic of both orally transmitted and multi-sourced compilations of wisdom sayings, as well as, mnemonic educative discourses and ordinary conversational speaking.

The *Tao Te Ching* text, as it as been historically named and as we presently know it, is, first and foremost, a 'Ching'. This means that, not only is it a classic text but, when the Chinese character 'Ching' is considered etymologically, it also is the flowing currents of underground watercourses, the longitudinal warp of loom weavings, the circuitous pathways of energetic meridians and the undergoing passages of living experiences.

Considering the content and themes of the *Tao Te Ching* as watercourses, weavings, circuits and passages; makes it easy to understand why the same waters, threads, energies and journeys are flowing, weaving, cycling and recurring in various and numerous places throughout the text.

In the *Tao Te Ching* text, there is a constant, consistent, continual and continuous energetic flowing, interweaving and passaging of the essential meanings of its multidimensional experiential concepts and existential themes. As the text is flowing, threading and passing along; there is not so much a change in content, form and meaning as there is an increase in the intensity, tempo and velocity of their application.

The Ultimate, Absolute, Eternal, Constant, mystical, metaphysical, transphenomenal, suprasensory and ineffable realities of Tao as Non-Being, One, Origin, Source and Mother and maxims regarding wise and harmonious ruling are generally somewhat more prevalent in earlier to middle passages (the *Tao Ching*); while middle to later passages (the *Te Ching*) generally focus somewhat more on the life-giving, life-sustaining, life-guiding, life-regulating and life-fulfilling Virtuosity, treasure and sanctuary of Tao as Heaven, Heaven-Earth and Nature and as embodied, personified and enacted by Sacred, wise, Tao-cultivating, Tao-according and Tao-identifying sages.

Flowing, weaving and passaging throughout the *Tao Te Ching* text are forms, attributes, characteristics, qualities and activities of Tao, e.g.,

1. Nothingness, pureness, oneness, groundedness, centeredness, clearness, emptiness, stillness, softness, openness, inclusiveness, greatness, spaciousness, vastness and wholeness.

2. Yin/Yang Ch'i dynamics of bipolarity, alternating, compensating, balancing, centering, voiding and reversing and paradoxes of human being, existence, consciousness, experience and living.

3. Wu Wei Ch'i kinetics of flowing, coursing, circulating, proceeding, unfolding, cycling and returning and water-like analogies in human being, existence, consciousness, experience and living.

4. Virtuosity/Te, Tao-nature, unique individuality and genius, integrity and authenticity, inner light and truth, potency and efficacy, trust and understanding, respect and honoring, humility and deference, frugality and moderation, accord and harmony, simplicity and sufficiency, nourishing and assisting, goodness and fairness, kindness and gentleness and matching Heaven, Heaven's Tao and Heavenly Tao.

5. Wu/Non-Being states of non-knowing (non- externalizing, abstracting, construing, defining, naming, interpreting, concluding etc.), non-having (non-desiring, evaluating, investing, seeking, pursuing, acquiring, attaching, etc.), non-doing (non-interfering, devising, implementing, controlling, forcing, aggressing,

contending, etc.) and non-being (non-distancing, separating, isolating, dividing, fragmenting, alienating,
excluding, etc.).

6. Yu/Being states of letting-be (awakening, witnessing,
   acknowledging, respecting, receiving, accepting, appreciating, etc.), letting-go (relinquishing, simplifying, aligning, attuning, adjusting, accomodating, according, etc.),
   going-with (yielding, acceding, allowing, responding,
   complying, following, accompanying, etc.) and being-
   with (associating, affiliating, allying, joining, connecting,
   participating, communing, etc.).

7. Tzu Jan/Wan Wu, the natural, spontaneous, automatic
   and free presencing of any and all of the myriad and
   diverse variety of unconceived, unintended, unplanned,
   serendipitous and surprising phenomena and happenings of human being, existence, consciousness, awareness and experience just *as* they are, of/*as* themselves so,
   just-so, *as*-such, *as*-is, self-so and self-like immanent,
   microcosmic and holographic correspondences of transcendent macrocosmic Tao.

8. Sheng Jen, Sacred and wise human beings who are Tao-
   focused and Tao-centered; Tao-embodied and Tao-
   personified; Tao-identified and Tao-like; egoless and
   universal; impartial and empathic; below and behind
   other human beings; soft and flexible; fluid and gentle;
   natural and spontaneous; responsible and helpful; living the 3 treasures of unconditioned love and coura-
   geousness, conserved resources and generousness and
   restrained precedence and splendidness; being Yin/Yang
   Ch'i-, Wu Wei Ch'i- and Tzu Jan-like, Tao- and Te-like,
   Heaven-like and a world treasure.

In its later passages, the intensity and momentum of the *Tao
Te Ching* keep building and accelerating; steadily, intrepidly and
almost fiercely; explicating the dehumanizing, inhuman and
fatal tragedies of our ignorance and error, daring and aggressing,

oppressing and violating, fighting and warring and killing and slaughtering instead of consciously and gratefully treasuring and safeguarding the blessed gift of our Sacred and precious human life. A crescendo is quietly, almost silently but nonetheless emphatically, reached in the final passage wherein the operation, workings and enactment of Heaven and the occupation, work and accomplishment of the sage are clearly and sharply identified and precisely and succinctly stated.

Far out in the great, vast and radiant splendor of Tao's Heaven is the providential originating, conducting, sustaining, regulating, executing, transforming, harmonizing, evolving and completing of our precious human life. And deep within the wise, open and awakened heart of Tao's sage is the quintessential Light, Reality, Truth, Beauty, Harmony, Grace, Peace, Joy and Love of our conscious human living.

The last lines of the *Tao Te Ching*'s climactic passage 81 are the conclusion, completion, consummation and culmination of its ancient message and long-standing transmission to us about what is ultimately fundamental and intimately significant in human being and being human ..... stated so sheerly and utterly, so purely and simply, and in so few words:

> *Heaven's Tao is benefiting, not harming*
> *Human Beings' Tao is assisting, not contending*

53. The phenomenological attitude and approach applied to wise psychotherapy/counseling entails wise attenders suspending/putting in abeyance/bracketing out (the epoche) past clinical experience, similar 'cases'; and treatment assumptions, presuppositions, preconceptions and expectations in order to be open 1) to receiving the 'givenness' of human beings entering into and engaging in psychotherapy/counseling and 2) to working within their absolutely unique subjective experiential frames of reference.

Technically, phenomenology is a philosophical discipline mostly considered as a 'pre-scientific' and descriptive pre-condition of/for serious inquiry and controlled experimentation according to orthodox scientific research procedures. However, in actual clinical experience, adopting a phenomenological attitude and approach has proven to be very effective as a psychotherapeutic 'treatment' in and of itself which has been identified by this practitioner as 'therapeutic phenomenology'. The closest parallel among traditional psychotherapy/counseling 'schools' is that of unconditional positive regard, organismic valuing and trust, congruent relating and accurate empathic reflecting in Non-Directive/Client/Person-Centered Therapy.

54. In a companion book entitled *Lao-Tzu's Tao Te Ching: Soul-Journeying Commentaries. A Sojourning Pilgrim's Rendering of 81 Spirit Soul Passages,* all of the passages are considered literally as transformative Soul-making/enSouling passages in/of our Human Soul's life-long Soul-work and Soul-journeying from ego to Spirit.

55. For related materials, references to Chinese Taoist philosophy, Taoism, the *Tao Te Ching* and Lao Tzu; Tao, Ch'i, Te, Yin Yang, Wu Wei and Tzu Jan; letting-be, letting-go, going-with and being-with; non-knowing, non-having, non-doing and non-being; transcendence, nonduality, nothingness and emptiness; Being, Psyche, Spirit and Soul; awakening, awareness, accepting and allowing; naturalness, spontaneity, presence and openness; balance, centeredness, oneness and wholeness; changing, transforming, unfolding and flowing and not-interfering, not-controlling, not-manipulating and not-forcing are explicitly made by, and can be found in the various writings of, phenomenologically, experientially, existential-humanistically and transpersonally-oriented psychoanalysts, psychiatrists, psychologists, psychotherapists, therapists and counselors such as Roberto Assagioli, Ludwig Binswanger, Jean Bolen, James Bugental, Erich Fromm, Georg Groddeck, John Heider, Thomas Hora, Carl Jung, Ron Kurtz, Alexander Lowen, Abraham Maslow, Rollo May, Fritz Perls, Carl Rogers, Wilson Van Dusen, Joseph Zinker, et al. And, of course, you can find and access materials integrating Chinese Taoism and psychotherapy using currently available on-line search engines.

APPENDIX ONE

81 Questions for Lao Tzu: a Fable

The following are 81 questions being asked of Lao Tzu by Yin Hsi, Guardian of the Han-Ku mountain pass, prior to Lao Tzu's journeying westward out of China sometime during the 6th-5th Centuries BCE.

Lao Tzu and Yin Hsi are sitting cross-legged on two flat rocks facing each other. A gentle breeze is fanning the warm shade of a late afternoon sun. Yin Hsi is asking Lao Tzu a series of 81 questions; some general, some specific, some clarifying, some associations from previous ones, some repeated and others random. Yin Hsi's questioning is thoughtful, for he is knowing that Lao Tzu's answers will only be as good and wise as the questions that he is being asked.

The question and answer meeting is completed in a single uninterrupted sitting and is concluded at dusk. While a pot of fresh herbal tea is resting and brewing atop a nearby burner, neither Yin Hsi nor Lao Tzu are partaking of any, staying fully absorbed in the matters at hand. Yin Hsi is dutifully inking Lao Tzu's answers to his questions on bamboo slips that he is bundling up and tying together. These answers later became known as the *Book of Lao Tzu* and the *Tao Te Ching*.

While recording Lao Tzu's words in approximately 5,000 Chinese characters, Yin Hsi is parenthetically experiencing succinct phrases deep within his heart-mind. The 81 questions and Yin Hsi's concise inner voices are given below. Lao Tzu's longer answers are the respective 81 *Tao Te Ching* passages given in this rendition.

1. Can Tao be known? *(Objectifying its Ultimate Reality is its immanent actuality.)*

2. Can anything be known? *(Through its bipolarity and complementarity.)*

3. How should life be lived? *(Through non-attachment and not interfering.)*

4. How can Tao be used? *(Let it operate and naturally compensate.)*

5. How does Tao work? *(Like the empty center of a bellows.)*

6. Who is the Valley Spirit? *(The Mysterious Feminine/ Root-Source.)*

7. Who are wise human beings? *(The universal/egoless ones.)*

8. What are they like? *(They are being like the goodness of water.)*

9. What is Heaven's Tao? *(Nothing extra/stopping in time/ withdrawing.)*

10. What is human Virtuosity? *(Inner Tao-nature/oneness/ suppleness/clearness.)*

11. What is most useful in life? *(The emptiness of inner/open/ center space.)*

12. What about sensory experience? *(Don't chase it/stay with inwardness.)*

13. What are favor and self like? *(They bring fear/trouble.)*

14. How can Tao be experienced? *(Through embodying and identifying as it.)*

15. Are Tao-Masters being so? *(They are careful/yielding/ natural/open/pure.)*

16. What is returning to Tao? *(Clearness/emptiness/stillness/ naturalness.)*

17. What about leaders? *(True ones are barely being known.)*

18. What happens if Tao is forgotten? *(Progressive degeneration.)*

19. How can Tao be taught? *(It can be modeled and transmitted.)*

20. How are you different? *(By being nourished by Mother Tao.)*

21. More about Virtuosity? *(It is uniquely individualizing Tao.)*

22. What is embodying One? *(Cycling/yielding/emptying/having little.)*

23. Is Tao like Nature? *(It is identical to it and Heaven-Earth.)*

24. What about human nature? *(Excessive/wasteful activities.)*

25. Is there a Tao-nature? *(It is greatness/spontaneity/Virtuosity.)*

26. How can Tao be remembered? *(By being grounded/centered.)*

27. How are wise human beings models? *(By following Inner Light.)*

28. What is Inner Light? *(Originality/ultimacy/naturalness.)*

29. What are leaders doing? *(Extremes/excesses/extravagances.)*

30. How can they use Tao? *(By not controlling/forcing/fighting.)*

31. What else can they do? *(Use their power to stop warfare.)*

32. What if they embodied Tao? *(Sweet simplicity/equality.)*

33. How would people develop? *(Being content/becoming immortal.)*

34. Would Tao be in the world then? *(Greatly so/flowing everywhere.)*

35. Is Tao like a magnet? *(An unseen centering force-field.)*

36. Is Tao paradoxical? *(Its bipolarity is naturally compensatory.)*

37. Does Tao 'do' anything? *(Just its natural seamless activity.)*

38. Does Virtuosity 'do' anything? *(It acts like Tao without need to do.)*

39. Can Oneness be experienced? *(As its many/diverse manifestations.)*

40. How does Tao operate? *(By the reversing/returning of Ch'i energy.)*

41. Can Tao be practiced? (*Few are. Its greatness appears in paradoxes.*)

42. Do you have a teaching? (*It is essentially non-violence.*)

43. More paradoxes? (*Teaching/practicing without speaking/acting.*)

44. That's non-doing. What about non-having? (*Being sufficient.*)

45. More paradoxes? (*Complete/sufficient may appear incomplete/insufficient.*)

46. What about insufficiency? (*Enough already! It is a tragedy.*)

47. What about seeking? (*Same thing. It is based upon insufficiency.*)

48. What is the way to sufficiency? (*Decreasing/simplifying.*)

49. What about preferences? (*Virtuosity is being impartial.*)

50. What is the benefit of not striving? (*Invulnerability.*)

51. Are Tao and Virtuosity enough? (*Honor and cherish them.*)

52. Is Tao like a good Mother? (*There is no danger.*)

53. Is everything Tao? (*Some deviations are not cultivating Tao.*)

54. Is Virtuosity cultivated? (*By being rooted in/connected with Tao.*)

55. What is harmony? (*Flexibility/vitality/according with Tao.*)

56. What is according with Tao? (*Identifying as the treasure of Tao.*)

57. What is Tao-identified ruling? (*Letting others be as they are.*)

58. More about ruling? (*Be unobtrusive/not invasive.*)

59. How can Virtuosity be developed? (*By conserving/compounding.*)

60. How does one govern by Tao? (*Not like dead rulers/live sages.*)

61. What marks a well developed state? (*Being lower/feminine.*)

62. Is Tao a precious Treasure? (*The world's greatest one.*)

63. What does a wise leader do? *(Address matters/issues early.)*

64. Say more? *(Then they are easy but that is difficult.)*

65. What makes it difficult? *(Too much sophistication.)*

66. Then what does a wise leader do? *(Stay below and behind.)*

67. What are the 3 Treasures of Tao? *(Frugality/compassion/ humility.)*

68. What about the military? *(Not coerce/contend/fight/hurt.)*

69. What about 'enemies'? *(No enemies/no fight/save treasures.)*

70. Do you have a practice? *(Living deep inner understanding.)*

71. What is this understanding? *(Not acting all-knowing.)*

72. Something more? *(Let everything be/respect the awesome.)*

73. Does all this take courage? *(Heaven's Tao is beyond courage.)*

74. What about dying? *(Accept the inevitability of Tao's working.)*

75. What else? *(Treasure the sheer/utter reality of living.)*

76. What marks living beings? *(Softness/flexibility/fluidity.)*

77. Again, what is Heaven's Tao? *(Compensating/counter balancing.)*

78. Can we really be soft and fluid? *(Yes, trust me on this one!.)*

79. Is living really all good? *(Yes, Heaven's Tao is impartial.)*

80. Is there really a Tao-topia? *(Yes, there is purely and simply.)*

81. You have answered a lot of questions and spoken a lot of true words that I cannot argue with. Is there any other wisdom that you might be imparting as we are completing our conversing? *(Do not accumulate for yourself. Give and use who you are and what you have to and for other human beings. Assist and benefit other human beings and do not contend with or harm them. Be Heavenly Tao.)*

Yin Hsi slowly stands up, bows humbly and thankfully and asks Lao Tzu a final question. 'Now, may I offer you some tea?' Lao Tzu respectfully bows, looks into Yin Hsi's eyes and nods agreement. And so it is, that Yin Hsi and Lao Tzu commiserate through the night under a clear starry sky, until the dawning sunrise, conversing about matters apparently not worthy of recording. After a brief rest, Yin Hsi decides to abandon his passkeeping post and to continue the journey with Lao Tzu, his newly found Spiritual friend and wayfaring companion. They both share some seeds of longevity, mount Lao Tzu's ox, proceed through the pass westward to the K'un Lun mountain of immortality and are never seen again.

APPENDIX TWO

Quick Reference to the 81 Experiences

The following is a concise quick reference to some of the awarenesses, attitudes, approaches and activities of wise psychotherapeutic attenders and of some of the characteristics, qualities, constituents and ingredients of the wise psychotherapeutic attending relationship/process gleaned from each one of the 81 *Tao Te Ching* experiences, synopses and commentaries of this rendition.

1. Not reductionistic abstracting/objectifying/defining/labeling.

2. Bipolar complementarity/attending/listening/supporting/assisting.

3. Not preferred theories/clever interpretations/crafty interventions.

4. Allow process to naturally unfold/spontaneously self-adjust.

5. Be in empty heart center with impartiality/equality/few words.

6. Identify as feminine/deep/receptive/nourishing/renewing.

7. Have no self-interest/identify as universal Self/step aside.

8. Be water-like/deep/flowing/yielding/sustaining/benefiting.

9. Maintain open space/solid edge/not overdo or pride in work/step back.

10. Conserve energy/not control/force/manipulate/interfere.

11. Integrate benefit of solid outer structure/utility of empty inner space.

12. Deeper inner organismic experience/not external sensory stimulation.

13. Value true Self/not ego/not favorite theories/techniques/ human beings.

14. Identify with transpersonal source of the regulating process.

15. Be awake/aware/attentive/open/yielding/accepting/ allowing.

16. Clear mind/empty heart/still will/witness cycling/ reversing/returning.

17. Be low profile/trust in process/limit verbalizing/ interfering.

18. Not intellectualizing/dehumanizing/being 'right'/doing 'good'.

19. Not being dogmatic/lecturing/crafting strategies/striving for successes.

20. Not judgments/planned agendas/purposeful objectives/ specific outcomes.

21. Be unique/efficacious potency of presence/gifts/ Virtuosity/genius.

22. Not assert positions/display talents/contend issues/parade successes.

23. Not extended monologues/lengthy interpretations/ prolonged interventions.

24. Not striving for insights/catharses/changes/ breakthroughs/'cures'.

25. Follow the natural/spontaneous coursing/developing/ completing of processs.

26. Stay grounded/centered amid possible distractions/ diversions.

27. Concise/clear/contactful/connected/complete interpretations/interactions.

28. Integrate feminine-masculine/unconscious-conscious/ body-Spirit.

29. Not control/manipulate bipolar alternating/reversing dynamic processes.

30. Not use force that results in conflicts/power struggles/ early termination.

31. Not wage war on issues using arsenals of techniques/ tactics/campaigns.

32. Not only use psychodiagnostic labels/psychopathological classifications.

33. Yield to the sufficiency/longevity of deeper/essential nature/Virtuosity.

34. Be supportive/not attached/dominating/claiming credit/ seeking fame.

35. Magnetically create an in-fluence of safety/stability/ security/serenity.

36. Be soft/tender/mild/gentle/flexible/yielding/humble/ modest.

37. Allow natural/spontaneous transforming without interfering.

38. Not need to 'do' or display gifts/talents/abilities/skills/ genius/Virtuosity.

39. Be nondual/integral/unitary/whole/balanced/humble/ ordinary.

40. Be soft/yielding/allowing experiences to arise/cycle/ reverse/return.

41. Wholeheartedly cultivate a psychospiritual practice/accept paradoxes.

42. Integrate/harmonize bipolar vital energies without aggressing/violating.

43. Do less purposeful verbalizing/acting/interfering/ intervening.

44. Not strive for name/fame/gain at the expense of being sufficient.

45. Open to the sufficiency/infallibility/inexhaustibility of natural law/energy.

46. Not compare to/compete with professional colleagues and their practices.

47. Understand the essence of human beings through inner experiencing.

48. Simplify treatment plans/intervention strategies into doing no-'things'.

49. Suspend fixed theoretical concepts/empathize with direct experience.

50. Identify with living/develop immunity to attack/harm/ injury.

51. Honor/cherish essential inner nature as nourishing/ sustaining/developing.

52. Relate to human beings as mothers/fathers/sisters/ brothers/children.

53. Not be diverted by fascinating histories/stories/ experiences/phenomena.

54. Experience the radial circles of selves/families/ communities/nations.

55. Cultivate original/natural integrity/flexibility/innocence/ harmony.

56. Not lose vital energy in intellectualizing and sensory experiencing.

57. Be open/straightforward without using clever/contrived strategies.

58. Be subdued/unobtrusive/not overbearing/overwhelming/ invasive.

59. Make concise/economical/efficient interpretations/ interactions/interventions.

60. Not be hindered/harmed by supernatural introjects or projections.

61. Be a low/deep/still/receptive/feminine converging point.

62. Not abandon human beings with undeveloped consciousnesses.

63. Address issues before full blown through early intervening.

64. Address issues before arising through preventative maintenance.

65. Restore the original simplicity of/not try to enlighten human beings.

66. Elevate/advance human beings by being below and behind them.

67. Treasure conserved resources, unconditioned love/ restrained precedence.

68. Not act-out negative transference projections and projective identifications.

69. Not assertively confront/aggressively attack defenses/ resistance/issues.

70. Consider the attending relationship as an intersubjective synchronicity.

71. Not act all-knowing even though well-versed in theories/ techniques.

72. Respect the awesomeness of human life/not oppress human beings.

73. Maintain the open spaciousness of awareness/attention without striving.

74. Not take over for the agency/operations/execution of natural laws.

75. Not be overtaxing/overcontrolling/overpowering/ overwhelming.

76. Maintain soft/flexible/fluid structure/limits/boundaries.

77. Assist human beings in counterbalancing deficiencies/ insufficiencies.

78. Use softness/gentleness in relating to/working with defenses/resistances.

79. Take full responsibility in agreements/conflicts without blaming others.

80. Be content with the simplicity/sufficiency of ordinary/ everyday human living.

81. Serve/assist/benefit human beings without contending with/harming them.

APPENDIX THREE

An Encounter Between a Taoist Sage and a Psychotherapist: Another Fable

TS Hey! Where are you headed?

AP To my office to meet with a new patient.

TS What will you be doing?

AP Well, first I'm going to be doing an intake interview to see what the presenting issues are, get some personal history, make some behavioral observations, make a diagnostic assessment and begin to theorize about her issues.

TS Oh, basically to see what's going on. Then what?

AP Well, then I'll be doing a clinical evaluation and case formulation; appraising her ego-defenses, strengths and weaknesses and using my clinical judgment about how to proceed in line with other past cases I've treated with similar issues.

TS Oh, simply to see what she wants to let change. Then what?

AP Well, then I'll get into some treatment planning, appraising coping skills and resources, starting to set some goals, getting some more ideas about how to proceed, doing some intervention strategizing and considering some techniques that I like to use.

TS Oh, actually to see how she might let things change. Then what?

AP Well, then I'll decide how often to meet, proceed with the treatment and then do an outcome evaluation to see if it worked and whether it's time for end-setting and determining termination.

TS Oh, finally to see if changes happened for her. Then what?.

AP   Well, I don't know what all of the issues are or how long all of this will take. I know from her phone message that she really is not in very good shape to deal with her life. She may need a medical workup, psychiatric referral, medication, hospitalization or longer term psychotherapy. I'll have to find out when I see her.

TS   I'm not a psychotherapist but, regardless of what's going on, and I'm not saying that this is the solution, I know that human beings benefit a great deal from validation, support and encouragement by trusting and experiencing that they really are okay, whole, free and open just as they naturally are. It can make all the difference and sometimes their concerns simply melt or fade away in light of such a given perspective.

AP   Well, I don't think that she feels that way about herself.

TS   Do you feel that way about her, at least in principle and, hopefully, in practice?

AP   Well, I don't know her yet, so I can't say.

TS   When you two meet, ask her about the ways she already feels that she is naturally okay, whole, free and open. It's very validating, integrating, transforming, liberating, empowering and enlivening to remember and to re-experience this about yourself.

AP   Well, in your experience that all may be true, well and good, but, as a way of working with her, I don't think it will somehow magically and automatically solve anything.

TS   Believe me. When someone whom you respect, value and trust really reminds you simply that you are a human being, you are alive, you are real, you are valid, you are here-now and you are who you are just as you are and that all of that is a wonderful blessing, precious gift and beautiful treasure; it has a very powerful influence and profound effect on their Heart and Soul and restores their dignity and worth as a significant human being. It's a much deeper and larger picture that kind of puts everything else in a relative, proper, more meaningful and less discouraging perspective and a fundamentally and essentially Spiritual context.

AP Well, I don't know what to say. I'd like to believe you, but in my profession we just go about dealing with people in a different way. She's coming to see a psychotherapist for help. She needs a diagnosis so her insurance will cover treatment. Managed health care limits the total number of sessions I have to see her. And explicit case formulations, treatment plans and progress notes are required and reviewed. That's just how it works. That's just how we have to do things.

TS I understand and wish you both well. Many times it's not easy being a real and truly human being, especially these days. Be good, kind, fair and gentle with yourself, her and the other human beings with whom you have the great honor and special opportunity to attend to, care for and to assist in the living of their lives. Everything should turn out okay in the long run or, maybe, even in the short run.

AP Well, thanks anyhow. I really have to go now. I can't be late for my session.

TS You take care now. Okay?

AP Okay. Bye.

TS Bye.

EPILOGUE

The following is a final note on the nature of some characteristics, qualities and psychotherapeutic applications of the *Tao
Virtuosity Experience*, as this rendition is so titled.

Tao as Clearness

Clearness is not the experience of clarity but the clearness of
experiencing. It is not the absence of image but is the perfectly
matched/reflected mental space of Te, e.g., when object and
image are veridical. Clearness is co-incidence at its maximum
potential for discerning image. It is the dustless mirror of Mind
that receives and accepts without retaining.

Wise attenders are awake and aware and their mental clear-
ness/clarity is not clouded over by analytic abstractions, theoretical concepts and diagnostic assessments. They are 'letting-be'
human beings and the attending relationship/process is one of
witnessing, acknowledging and reflecting.

Tao as Emptiness

Emptiness is not the experience of vacuity but the emptiness of experiencing. It is not the absence of form but is the
perfectly matched/balanced emotional center of Yin/Yang Ch'i,
e.g., when two objects of equal weight placed on the pans of a
scale appear neutral.

Emptiness is the dynamic plenum void at its maximum
potential for manifesting form. It is the bottomless vessel of
Heart that resonates and accords without revising.

Wise attenders are attuned and accorded and their emotional
emptiness/vacuity is not filled up with formulaic evaluations,

preferred interpretations and clinical judgments. They are 'letting-go' human beings and the attending relationship/process is one of equalizing, balancing and centering.

Tao as Stillness

Stillness is not the experience of tranquility but the stillness of experiencing. It is not the absence of movement but is the perfectly matched concurrent volitional source of Wu Wei Ch'i, e.g., when riding in one and looking at the other of two adjacent vehicles traveling in the same direction at the same speed it appears stationary. Stillness is the kinetic plenum stasis at its maximum potential for mobilizing form. It is the timeless ground of Body that responds and allows without resisting.

Wise attenders are allowing and following and their volitional stillness/tranquility is not busied with contrived purposes, methodological techniques and strategic interventions. They are 'going-with' human beings and the attending relationship/process is one of unfolding, proceeding and developing.

Tao as Oneness

Oneness is not the experience of unity but the oneness of experiencing. It is not the absence of being but is the perfectly matched/co-existing relational identity of One Tao, e.g., when two individual human beings empathically experience their universality and appear identical. Oneness is commonality at its maximum potential for experiencing uniqueness. It is the endless circle of Being that returns and abides without regressing.

Wise attenders are affiliated and allied and their relational oneness/unity is not separated by distancing objectifications, alienated relationships and disconnected interactions. They are 'being-with' human beings and the attending relationship/process is one of intersubjectivity, connection and communion.

Tao as Pureness

Pureness is not the experience of purity but the pureness of experiencing. It is not the absence of objects but is the perfectly matched/equalized phenomenal diversity of Wan Wu, e.g., when all of the rich and varied myriad objects of experience are amalgamated. Pureness is absoluteness at its maximum potential for experiencing relativity. It is the matchless waters of Experience that restore and array without receding.

Wise attenders are absolute and merged and their essential pureness/purity is not mixed up with confused interpretations, hasty associations and adulterated procedures. They are 'being-as' human beings and the attending relationship/process is one of validity, diversity and integrity.

Tao as Wholeness

Wholeness is not the experience of totality but the wholeness of experiencing. It is not the absence of parts but is the perfectly matched/fitting existential entirety of Ch'i, e.g., when all of the discrete pieces of life and experience are suitable. Wholeness is allness at its maximum potential for experiencing constituents. It is the boundless space of Consciousness that reanimates and energizes without requiring.

Wise attenders are comprehensive and complete and their existential wholeness/totality is not fragmented by reductionistic distinctions, incomplete understandings and partial interpretations. They are 'being-all' human beings and the attending relationship/process is one of consummation, culmination and fulfillment.

Tao as Freeness

Freeness is not the experience of liberty but the freeness of experiencing. It is not the absence of limits but is the perfectly matched/conformed natural spontaneity of Tzu Jan, e.g., when unrestrained expression appropriately complies with necessities. Freedom is unlimitedness at its maximum potential for experiencing boundaries. It is the central fire of Self that recreates and appears without replaying.

Wise attenders are unconfined and presencing and their situational freeness/liberty is not bound up by limited possibilities, behavioral constraints and rehearsed performances. They are 'being-so' human beings and the attending relationship/process is one of Self-creating, Self-presencing and Self-soness.

Tao as Naturalness

Naturalness is not the experience of non-artificiality but the naturalness of experiencing. It is not the absence of artificiality but is the perfectly matched/actuality of Sheng Jen, e.g., wherein the ordinary and extraordinary, the everyday and rare the usual and exceptional and Nature and culture are embodied and personified by Sacred/wise human beings. Naturalness is reality at its maximum potential for being everyone and living everywhere. It is the sheer and utter innocence of the Child who reincarnates and amazes without relenting.

Wise attenders are ordinary and everyday and their ontological naturalness is not displaced by impersonal relationships, unsustainable requirements and engineered effects. They are 'being-living' human beings and the attending relationship/process is one of freshness, vitality and vibrancy.

Tao as Openness

Openness is not the experience of availability but the openness of experiencing. It is not the absence of closedness but is the perfectly matched/creative open matrix of Original Tao, e.g., when all life experiences rhythmically appear, are undergone and then disappear with equality and impartiality. Openness is availability at its maximum potential for experiencing the hiddenness of Mystery. It is the swinging Gate of Spirit that reveals and avails without regretting.

Wise attenders are available and accessible and their original openness is not closed off by definitive interpretations, final conclusions and unmodifiable prognoses. They are 'being-x' human beings and the attending relationship/process is one of entering, exiting and transitioning.

Clearing Mind, emptying Heart, stilling Will, unifying Being, purifying Experience, integrating Consciousness, liberating Self, beholding Spirit and enjoying Life constitute the Ground, Center and Spaciousness of the Soul-Journeying and Tao-Wayfaring of Human Being and Being Human.

Wise attenders have perfectly assimilated and fully integrated their innate gifts, talents and genius with their acquired technical skills, competencies and proficiences into/*as* the Virtuosity, natural spontaneity, creative artistry, harmonious potency and appropriate efficacy of their personal and professional human being, living and 'doings' in and throughout the attending relationship/process of their psychotherapy/counseling practice, i.e., their 'great technical skill in the practice of a fine art'.

T'AI   CHI

SUPREME	ULTIMATE
HIGHEST	ACME/APEX/SUMMIT/ZENITH
GREATEST	GREATEST EXTENT
FARTHEST/EXTREME	UTMOST EXTREMITY
VERY/EXCEEDINGLY	VERY/EXCEEDINGLY
EPITHET FOR EXCELLENCE	FIRST PRINCIPLE/THE POLES

The T'ai Chi/Supreme Ultimate symbol depicts the balancing, interacting and unifying of Heaven-Earth, Yin/Yang Ch'i energies and all bipolarities within human being, existence and experience. T'ai Chi is synonymous with Tao/the Supreme One/Primordial Unity and Original/Primordial Ch'i. The symbol combines Wu Chi, the limitless/nonultimate/ undifferentiated Reality and the Great Yin/Yang Ch'i/bipolar energies which together originate Heaven-Earth, Human Beings and the '10,000 things' of the material and phenomenal worlds.

T'ai Chi is also depicted as a ridgepole, the highest point of a building, that which is between all that is below and above it; again, symbolizing the integrating and uniting of the Earthly and Heavenly realms as well as the physical and Spiritual Souls of human beings. Experiencing the Reality of T'ai Chi is a concluding, completing, consummating and culminating end-point of human being, existing and living.

Tao as T'ai Chi

T'ai Chi is the Supreme Ultimate/Great Extreme/Ultimate Limit and identical with Tao. In the cosmogonic sequencing of Reality, Wu Chi, the primordial undifferentiated Ultimateless, differentiates into Primordial Ch'i energy which further differentiates into Yin Ch'i and Yang Ch'i energies which originate Heaven, Earth and Human Being; the physical/P'o and the Spiritual/Hun twin Human Souls and the 10,000 things/Wan Wu of Life, all of which are immanent holographic microcosms of transcendent Tao.

T'ai Chi is the living symbol of the co-existing, alternating, counterbalancing, centering, voiding and reversing dynamic bipolarity of Yin/Yang Ch'i energies at their maximum potential to either 'Yin' into empty, still and deep inner space or to 'Yang' into full, moving and surface outer forms and to manifest the countless qualities of either Yin Ch'i or Yang Ch'i energies.

The T'ai Chi symbol depicts the reality that Yin/Yang Ch'i energies are inherent in their bipolar complements. Each exists within the other and contains its complement within itself. The T'ai Chi symbol affords a visual representation of the reality that health is latent within illness and vice versa, that there is a patient/counselee within the psychotherapist/counselor and vice versa and that their relationship is a dyadic bipolar and dynamically interacting Yin/Yang Ch'i unit.

It has been amply demonstrated that when psychotherapists/counselors are present with patients/counselees and are embodying the states of clearness, emptiness, stillness, oneness, pureness, wholeness, freeness, naturalness and openness as described above; patients/counselees are naturally more clearly aware, fully contacted, self-initiating, deeply connected, self-disclosing, wholly integrated and open to, and free to be, their natural and authentic selves. Wise psychotherapy/counseling is most efficient and effective when psychotherapists/counselors can find and experience and empathize and identify with patients/counselees within themselves and vice versa.

The T'ai Chi symbol offers a model for revisioning and resolving dualistic or conflicted relationships through mutually inclusive both/and bipolar integrations rather than through mutually exclusive either-or dualistic separations. Such a bipolar state of being is one where unique counterparts are co-existing; mutual, complementary and equal and reciprocally interacting, interchanging and co-operating within a transpersonal context without being dualistic, antagonistic and conflicting opposites.

In such a world of *human* beings, there would be no 'others' who are rivals, adversaries, contenders, opponents, antagonists, enemies, strangers, foreigners or aliens to fear, compete with, fight against, defeat, convert or eliminate. Bipartisan politics would be transpartisan; disputed national boundaries would be shared interfaces; unfair trade practices would be bilaterally beneficial; discriminated and stratified racial and ethnic groups, genders and social classes would be impartially and equally integrated; warring factions and peoples would co-exist peacefully, cooperate harmoniously, collaborate synergistically and co-create productively as planetary sisters and brothers in a universal human community and so-called 'alien' extraterrestrial beings would probably interact with us more frequently, visibly and naturally, etc..

Meditating on the Great Image of the T'ai Chi symbol and practicing the moving meditations of T'ai Chi Ch'uan/Supreme Ultimate Boxing and Ch'i Kung/Vital Energy Work, either individually or especially in small groups, are gentle and graceful ways of 1) awakening consciousness of the identity of Ultimate Reality and the intimate actualities of ordinary being and everyday living and 2) promoting:

❖ Earth/Belly/Heart- grounded/focused/centered conscious awareness.

❖ physical strength/balance/flexibility/fluidity/health/

      immunity/longevity.

❖   mental concentration/stability/clarity/acuity/insight/
discernment/peace.

❖   emotional simplicity/acceptance/security/confidence/
well-being/happiness.

❖   social interrelation/interconnection/interaction/
equality/impartiality/community.

❖   Spiritual awareness/faith/trust/transformation/
development/freedom.

and, hence, optimizing the human experiencing of being and living, sharing and enjoying the blessed gift, precious treasure and splendid opportunities of our ephemeral incarnation on Earth as Sacred Human Beings, Selves, Souls and Spirits.

This wayfaring counselor's rendering of Lao Tzu's *Tao Te Ching*, here considered as the *Tao Virtuosity Experience*, has been a special honor and heartwarming joy to complete and contribute as part of an over two-thousand year lineage of many hundreds of translations, commentaries and adaptations made by devoted and dedicated Taoist masters and disciples, teachers and students and scholars and practitioners for the benefit of fellow human beings. This work has been especially meaningful to/for me as a way of completing a richly rewarding life-long personal journey, lengthy professional vocation, Soulful voyage and Spiritual odyssey.

As stated in the conclusion of the Introduction to this rendition, if this material is in some, or any, way of interest, value, encouragement, support, assistance, guidance, use and/or benefit to you in awakening, discovering, experiencing, understanding and sharing your precious human being, conscious human living and unique wayfaring journeying; I am infinitely pleased and eternally grateful.

CODA

Lao Tzu's *Tao Virtuosity Experience/Tao Te Ching* is the first volume of a *Taoist Trilogy* that includes Chuang Tzu's *Interior Records/Nei P'ien* and Lieh Tzu's *Nature of Real Living/Hsing Shih Sheng*. The adages and commentaries of the *Tao Virtuosity Experience/Tao Te Ching* describe the nature, qualities, attributes, activities and relationships of Wise Human Beings/Sheng Jen and of wise attenders who are conducting the attending relationship/process of psychotherapy/counseling; both of whom are embodying, personifying, enacting and modeling a way of human being/living that is identified with/*as* Tao, its dynamic-kinetic Yin/Yang Ch'i and Wu Wei Ch'i operations and its spontaneous presencing/Tzu Jan *as* the experiential phenomena/Wan Wu of/in their awakened consciousness, awareness and experience.

Identifying with the Spirit, Heart and Soul of Lao Tzu and with Wise Human Beings/Sheng Jen and wise attenders, as characterized in the adages and commentaries of the *Tao Virtuosity Experience/Tao Te Ching;* opens the Way to ourselves being wise human beings and wise attenders who are attentively relating to human beings and who are being attentively related to by them. The Way is opened to being our own wise Selves and to wisely living our own lives in heartfelt, wholehearted and heartwarming ways that are more awake, conscious, balanced, harmonious, flowing, peaceful, intimate and fulfilling and that naturally and Sacredly integrate our Heavenly Spirit and our Earthly body *as* our Human Soul.

REFERENCES

Cleary, Thomas (Trans.). *The Taoist Classics:* Vol. 1. Boston: Shambhala Publications, Inc.. 1990.

Dainian, Zhang. *Key Concepts in Chinese Philosophy.* Edmund Ryden (Ed. & Trans.). New Haven: Yale University Press/ Beijing Foreign Languages Press. 2002.

Dong, Li. *Concise Chinese Dictionary: Chinese-English/English-Chinese.* Rutland, Vermont: Tuttle Publishing. 2015.

Feng, Gia-fu and English, Jane (Trans.). *Lao Tsu: Tao Te Ching.* New York: Vintage Books. 1972.

Fenn, C. H.. *The Five Thousand Dictionary: Chinese-English.* Cambridge: Harvard University Press. 1976.

Fischer-Schreiber, Ingrid. *The Shambhala Dictionary of Taoism.* Werner Wunsche (Trans.). Boston: Shambhala Publications, Inc.. 1996.

Heider, John. *The Tao of Leadership.* New York: Bantam Books. 1985.

Huang, Quanyu; Chen, Tong and Huang, Kuangyan. *McGraw-Hill's Chinese Dictionary and Guide to 20,000 Essential Words.* New York: McGraw-Hill. 2010.

Johanson, Greg and Kurtz, Ron. *Grace Unfolding: Psychotherapy in the Spirit of the Tao-Te Ching.* New York: Bell Tower. 1991.

Kluemper, Michael L. and Nadeau, Kit-Yee Yam. *Mandarin Chinese Characters Made Easy.* Rutland, Vermont: Tuttle Publishing. 2016.

Matthews, Alison and Matthews, Laurence. *Learning Chinese Characters.* Rutland, Vermont: Tuttle Publishing. 2007.

Matthews, R.H.. *Matthew's Chinese-English Dictionary.* Cambridge: Harvard University Press. 1943.

McNaughton, William and Ying, Lee. *Reading and Writing Chinese: Traditional Character Edition.* Rutland, Vermont: Tuttle Publishing. 1999.

Star, Jonathan (Trans. & Commentary). *Tao Te Ching: The Definitive Edition*. New York: Jeremy P. Tarcher/Putnam. 2001.

Watts, Alan and Huang, Al Chung-liang. *Tao: The Watercourse Way*. New York: Pantheon Books. 1975.

Watts, Alan. *What Is Tao?* Novato, California: New World Library. 2000.

Webster's New Collegiate Dictionary. Springfield, Massachusetts: G. & C. Merriam Co.. 1979.

Wieger, L.. *Chinese Characters: Their Origin, Etymology, History, Classification and Signification*. L. Davrout (Trans.). New York: Dover Publications, Inc.. 1966.

Wilder, G.D.. and Ingram, J.H.. *Analysis of Chinese Characters*. New York: Dover Publications, Inc.. 1974.

Wong, Eva. *Taoism: An Essential Guide*. Boston: Shambhala Publications, Inc.. 1997.

Wu, Yi. *Chinese Philosophical Terms*. Lanham, Maryland: University Press of America. 1986.

Wu, Yi. *The Book of Lao Tzu: The Tao Te Ching*. San Francisco: Great Learning Publishing Co.. 1989.

About the Author

Ray Vespe received his B.A. Psychology degree from Cornell University (1958), M.S. Clinical Psychology degree from Case Western Reserve University (1959) and Ph.D. Counseling Psychology degree from the California Institute of Integral Studies (1986). He has educated, trained, supervised, counseled and mentored graduate students in the Integral Counseling Psychology program at CIIS (1972-1990), the Transpersonal Psychology program at the California Institute of Transpersonal Psychology (1977-1979) and the Transpersonal Counseling Psychology program at John F. Kennedy University (1978-1990). Ray has worked in a wide variety of inpatient, outpatient, agency and group treatment settings and was Clinical Director of the Integral Counseling Center (1975-1978/1982-1990), San Leandro Community Counseling (1990-1992) and Marin Treatment Center (1992-2004). He has been a student of Tao for sixty-two years, has engaged in psychotherapy work for fifty-seven years and has maintained a licensed private practice for forty-four of those years. Ray is currently retired and living in Sonoma County, California.

Lightning Source UK Ltd.
Milton Keynes UK
UKHW020944150822
407319UK00011B/1892